BLACK WOMAN IN GREEN

BLACK WOMAN
IN GREEN

GLORIA BROWN
and the Unmarked Trail
to Forest Service
Leadership

Gloria D. Brown and Donna L. Sinclair

Oregon State University Press   Corvallis

Cataloging-in-publication data is available from the Library of Congress.

ISBN 978-0-87071-001-8 (paper)
ISBN 978-0-87071-005-6 (ebook)

♾ This paper meets the requirements of ANSI/NISO Z39.48-1992
(Permanence of Paper).

All photographs are from the collection of Gloria D. Brown unless noted.
Cover photograph of the Siuslaw National Forest by Will Sylwester | Adobe Stock.

 **Oregon State University**
OSU Press

Oregon State University Press
121 The Valley Library
Corvallis OR 97331-4501
541-737-3166 • fax 541-737-3170
www.osupress.oregonstate.edu

This book is dedicated to my partner for life, Phil Wikelund, and to all my children and grandchildren. —Gloria Brown

Contents

Foreword

IN THIS BEAUTIFULLY NARRATED ACCOUNT, Gloria Brown details her three-decade struggle to become the nation's first female African American forest supervisor. The inspiring story illuminates critical themes of the last decades of the twentieth century—especially how civil rights, feminist, and environmental movements influenced one of the most significant federal agencies in the West. It illustrates how the US Forest Service, long dominated by white men, led Brown on a personal journey that also helped transform the institution.

In 1981, suddenly required to become sole provider for her three children, Brown resolved to climb out of the US Forest Service transcription pool by seizing every opportunity the agency might offer. Timing worked on Brown's behalf: Title VII of the federal Civil Rights Act of 1964 prohibited employers from discriminating against employees on the basis of sex or race, and the 1972 Equal Employment Opportunity Act provided enforcement tools for women to challenge discrimination. Although the Forest Service, along with other male-dominated workplaces, resisted changing its culture, 1970s and 1980s legal challenges to the agency led to increased numbers of women employees. Still, in order to advance, Brown had to uproot her children and leave her well-established family and friend networks in Washington, DC, to move west, where the region's extensive Forest Service operations provided career progression prospects. Although a reluctant migrant, Brown moved in 1986 to Missoula's Region 1 for a public affairs position, and then to Region 6 in Portland, determined to move up professionally, as she said, in "a far whiter America than I'd ever seen before."

Racism and discrimination are realities seldom probed in the mythical West, but for people of color, fighting stereotypes and microaggressions are part of daily life in our workplaces and communities. Gloria Brown employed various strategies—including hard work, diplomacy, humor, and cultivating allies—to become accepted, respected, and rewarded for her talents. "It was never easy to be the only African American in the room, but it was common in the Forest Service West." The journey tested her, especially when confronting racist threats to her children—not to mention the challenges that all single parents face and the cultural isolation and whiteness of the Northwest. Brown persisted in her quest to earn promotions and greater responsibilities in the Forest Service, and for a time in the Bureau of Land Management, but her ambition came with personal costs. As for many women who struggle to care for families and advance their careers, Brown often had to make painful choices personally and professionally.

Along with growing strong relationships with new friends and colleagues, Brown came to love the mountains, forests, rivers, and shoreline of her Forest Service purview and the new skills acquired. She received training or experience in firefighting, packing, camping, preparing maps and briefing books, assisting Congress with wilderness legislation, providing diversity training, and interacting with officials and community members. As public affairs specialist for the Willamette National Forest, then in her training as a forester and advancement from assistant ranger on the Rigdon Ranger District to forest supervisor on the Siuslaw and Los Padres National Forests, she came to know and speak and write about all elements of Forest Service projects.

As Brown's occupational journey schooled her in the ecological diversity of the region, she observed and participated in major shifts at the Forest Service and debates over public land use. She faced controversies among various public interest groups and within the agency. New environmental ethics often put younger "ologists" in conflict with senior career employees over managing ecosystems and tree harvests, and environmental activists and timber communities became more impassioned about saving endangered species or timber jobs. Her balanced account reveals the complexities and challenges of the work—in what many might assume to be a dull bureaucracy—and the critical role of federal agencies in managing public lands.

By the 1990s, the Forest Service had doubled its number of female employees and hired almost 8 percent more people of color. As in other areas of US employment, however, just as underrepresented people gained access to coveted middle-class jobs thanks to antidiscrimination policies, those job opportunities began to shrink. Plagued by budget cuts and declining timber revenues, Region 6 lost almost half its employees. It was in this environment that Brown finally realized her "dream job" as forest supervisor for the Siuslaw National Forest, becoming in 1999 the first black woman to manage an entire national forest. As this reminiscence looks back, we glimpse through Brown's service the possibilities of a better society, where democratic management is practiced, various publics are included in decision making, and employers seek the diversity that reflects the nation. But by the late twentieth century, decreased federal domestic spending, including on management of public lands, reduced opportunities for women and people of color in the Forest Service and failed to curb workplace sexual harassment, as witnessed by some twenty-first-century high-profile cases in the agency.

Black Woman in Green reveals the power of oral history, autobiography, and intimate collaboration. Historian Donna Sinclair, who describes her role in this project as "storytelling facilitator," helped shape the narrative that we read of a fascinating and courageous lived history, a product of fruitful collaboration. I join others in gratitude to Gloria Brown and Donna Sinclair for this important contribution to the literature of western, women's, African American, and environmental history.

Laurie Mercier
Claudius O. and Mary W. Johnson Distinguished
Professor of History, Washington State University Vancouver

Preface

I MET GLORIA BROWN IN 2004, first through a recorded interview, the rich, steady timbre of her voice effecting a tone of intimacy as she deliberately remembered and called my student, Janice Waldron, by name. Janice had driven to Corvallis to interview Gloria for my Voices from the Forest class at Portland State University. A young African American woman herself, Janice had chosen Gloria as her interview subject because she was the first female African American forest supervisor in the United States. I clearly recall listening to Gloria's story, crying at the poignant parts and wondering how she could speak so calmly when describing her tribulations. At the time, Gloria, who had become supervisor of the Siuslaw National Forest five years earlier, in 1999, was on her way to managing a larger national forest in California.

I had taught this same class for several years, but this time was different. In 2001, my students interviewed former Forest Service workers from the 1920s and 1930s; the next year focused on former Civilian Conservation Corps members. These men—all white men—had strung telephone line, built trails and fire lookouts, replanted forests after major fires, and begun developing the infrastructure for the 193-million-acre National Forest System, established in 1905. Nearly a hundred years later (2003), my students interviewed another group of white men who built thousands of miles of road into those forests during and after World War II and made the Forest Service famous for harvesting billions of board feet of timber. In 2004, David Gross from the Workforce Diversity Council of the Forest Service, a committee I'd never before encountered, came to PSU and asked me to interview women and minorities. Retirement loomed for this Forest Service demographic, most of whom came to the agency around the same time as Gloria, during the 1970s.

By then, I knew a lot about the Forest Service, from its origins to the environmental battles of the 1990s. This familiarity with the white, male, and macho hundred-year-old agency made the stories of professional women, people of color, and those with disabilities striking. Tales from the Civil Rights Department often started with programs like the Youth Conservation Corps and Cooperative Education Program that facilitated entry of African American, Asian, and Latino students into the agency. The inclusion of people in wheelchairs had helped increase access to public lands, and African American scientists had created environmental programs for black and brown youth. By 2007, the Forest Service had its first female chief, Abigail Kimbell, a forester and engineer. But there was no one like Gloria Brown, a black woman from the East Coast who joined the Forest Service in a traditionally female position in 1974 and became the first black woman to take charge of a national forest twenty-five years later.

When Gloria started her Forest Service career in the Washington, DC, transcription pool, no women or African Americans had ever held the decision-making authority of line officer in the organization (district ranger, forest supervisor, regional forester, or agency chief). In this agency, known for its esprit de corps and technical efficiency grounded in Progressive Era origins, white male foresters ran a tight, hierarchical, self-supporting organization, funded by timber. But times had changed, and a host of environmental laws influenced national forest management in the late twentieth century. These stories of women and people of color showed that civil rights legislation also influenced Forest Service operations, shaping what I have called *entwined diversification*,[1] the process, first implemented during the 1970s and 1980s, of overlapping environmental and social legislation that has led to ecological, occupational, and social shifts in the Forest Service. For the first time, the agency hired women who weren't secretaries, people of color to work in professional positions, and "ologists" of many sorts. From biologists to archaeologists, the intersection between equal employment legislation and environmental law meant their presence overlapped with agency workforce diversification efforts.

In 1990, Herbert McLean noted that the Pacific Northwest "leads the pack" in re-gendering the US Forest Service, a forty-thousand-person agency that had more than doubled its number of female employees in the previous two decades. With a third of the agency's sixty female district rangers in the region, and still others moving into professional positions via the clerical pool or as direct hires, McLean provided sound advice for advancement: "Go West young woman."[2] Gloria Brown had already figured that out, heading west in 1986 in order to advance. "It was all about the money in those days," she once told me, "to feed those kids."[3] That theme encompasses the story that follows, as does Gloria's recognition that she had to advocate for herself, because no one else would. Gloria refused to believe she could not rise to the highest levels of the Forest Service, even if others didn't recognize her potential. That spirit of, "Yes, I can" permeated everything she did.

A complex set of conditions set the stage for Gloria's advancement, including other female "firsts" in the Northwest's national forests. But Gloria Brown is remarkable for several reasons. Her experience as a non-forester prepared her far better for management positions that required a public interface than forester training might have. She sought mentors, gained the required knowledge and skills to advance, and advocated for other women, and she credits those who worked for and with her. Finally, on the precipice of the twenty-first century, Gloria became the first black female forest supervisor in the country. Although her story does not skirt racism, she approaches the topic cautiously, reflecting a philosophy she carried into her work, one that illustrates her own temperament: always assume the best and give people a chance—a view that allowed her to exist, and even thrive, in overwhelmingly white environments.

While writing my dissertation, "Caring for the Land, Serving People: Creating a Multicultural Forest Service in the Civil Rights Era," I serendipitously encountered Gloria again. A friend of mine who met Gloria at a party told me I might want to talk with her for my research. I was very excited when I realized she was referring to the same woman I'd met once before through her voice, but never in person. After two interviews, Gloria decided she wanted to work with me to tell her story more broadly. We then set out on a journey that has included interviewing others and talking for hours in the car, as well as many more hours of recorded interview, walks on the beach, and home visits. We also spent hours and hours on FaceTime discussing language, reading sentences aloud, and expanding the narrative by recording verbal accounts to paper. The result is a book created through a process that mixes spoken and written word to tell the story of a woman and an organization, a mother and a society, a forester and a leader.

Donna Sinclair

April 7, 2019

Acknowledgments

First to my partner, Phil Wikelund, and the rest of my family, thank you for your love, patience, and support. Thanks Donna—without your help there would be no book. Thanks to all the women who supported me: Nancy Graybeal, FS; Elaine Zielinski, BLM. Marilyn Kerns, Barbara-Woods Ingersoll, you consoled by me when I cried and made me laugh when no one else could. Thank you, Teresa, Dale, and Jane, the three best gatekeepers a leader could have. Thank you to my Mount St. Helens staff—we accomplished a lot together, tackling issues ranging from Native American land exchanges to conflicts between conservationists and kayakers about river habitat restoration, all while operating three interpretive centers. Thanks to my Baker City staff who taught me how to manage a noncontiguous land base with ranchers, miners, and a world-class interpretive center. My first job as a forest supervisor surrounded me with the smartest staff and rangers around. They carried out my vision to leave the Siuslaw ecologically better for fish, wildlife, and our land base, by taking out dikes, closing roads, and restoring a significant river to its original meandering flow for fish. Last, for the many awards, including the nomination for the International Theiss award for river management, a heartfelt thank-you. I want to thank my staff and rangers on the Los Padres National Forest, especially my deputy forest supervisor, Ken Heffner. Ken, without you my job would have been much harder, especially when it came to the many fires we had.

I want to thank the men throughout my career whose shoulders I stood on: Tom Hamilton (deceased), Lamar Beasley, Arlen Roll, Bob Devlin, and Mike Kerrick.

Last I want to say thank-you to award winning author Richard Ford. When my worst-case scenario happened in Montana, Richard Ford, before he was famous, sent me a letter that captured exactly what I was feeling.

Gloria D. Brown

Mary Braun, I thank you for the many conversations at conferences, the frank discussion, walks on the beach, and the ongoing confidence you provided us both. You put us into good hands with OSU Press staff Tom Brown, Micki Reaman, and Marty Brown. Thank you. The careful copy editing of Susan Campbell also made finalizing the text and debating capitalization over email a lot of fun! I especially thank Janice Waldron who drove to Corvallis, Oregon, to interview Gloria in 2004. Little did this former student know as she literally went the extra mile that she would play a key role in telling Gloria's story. Johanna Ogden reconnected me with Gloria after serendipity brought them in contact in 2011. You have my hearty thanks, Jo, for always thinking about history, social justice, and your history sisters. To the many Forest Service employees who helped me to understand the agency, gender dynamics, and issues of race and place, I cannot thank you enough. It is because of you that Gloria and I worked so well together in crafting her narrative.

To Gloria: thank you for asking me to be your partner in this journey. I helped you to write it, but you did the hard work of living it.

Donna L. Sinclair

CHAPTER 1
A Good White-Collar Job

RELIGIOUS PEOPLE SAY THAT WHEN God closes one door, He opens another. People also say that if something doesn't kill you, it will make you stronger. I believe both of these statements, maybe because my parents took me to church from the time I was born, to the "little buds" choir, the junior choir, and to more sermons than I care to remember. To this day, my extended family still attends the quaint red-brick Russell Temple Methodist Church in Alexandria, Virginia, on South Alfred Street, with its twelve white steps and twelve windows tinted with heavenly symbols open to the sky. I used to daydream about my books, my life, and what I would be when I grew up while the pastor preached in the stuffy crowded house of worship. It was only when Willie James died that I stopped going to church and stopped daydreaming.

The hospital waiting room felt cold and sterile. *It's raining like cats and dogs and that's probably why I'm alone in this huge room,* I thought. *Only fools and drunk drivers would be out on a night like this! That's right, fools, including me. Why in God's name did I agree to attend class, especially tonight?* The morning had been disastrous. Our car keys were missing. *I know I hung them by the kitchen door!* This morning they were gone. We tore the house up, took dishes from cupboards, dish towels from drawers, and even emptied the silverware tray. We looked under and behind everything, threw clothes on the floor in every bedroom, but we ran out of time. The kids had to get to Holy Name Catholic School; we had to catch the bus. I was mad.

At the bus stop, my husband Willie James quizzed our middle daughter, Catrina, on her upcoming spelling test. I continued to fume. When I heard Willie James correct a word Catrina misspelled, I knew he was wrong, and we discussed the word all the way to the babysitter, where we dropped off the kids and caught the bus to downtown Washington, DC. It was September 1981; Willie James was a cement foreman for HHS Construction Company, and they were putting up a Marriott Hotel two blocks from the White House.

We got off at the same bus stop, and I walked up to Fourteenth and Independence, where the United States Department of Agriculture Forest Service (USFS) headquarters stood. The historic Romanesque-style building rose four stories high between two of the busiest streets in DC, Twelfth and Fourteenth. Its dark gray bricks, sterile and lifeless, made it look like a prison without barbed-wire fences, guards, and guns, but formidable nonetheless. I worked for the US Department of Agriculture in the Forest Service Office of Information and Education (I&E). I took calls from all over the United States and even overseas, on the main line for this government agency that managed the nation's 193 million acres of public forests and grasslands. That fated morning, I went straight to my desk, where I cheerfully answered, "Hello, Forest Service, Information and Publications. This is Gloria Brown. May I help you?" People called to ask for all kinds of things: the brochure, whether Smokey the Bear could visit a school, or whether they could ski in the Mount Hood National Forest or go whitewater rafting in a national forest. It was 1981, and my office was on the third floor, the same level as the chief of the Forest Service, the engineer Max Peterson.

My first job with USFS was as a GS-4 dictating machine transcriber, a DMT.[1] I had passed the civil service exam and could have worked in any of several agencies: Forest Service, Department of Housing and Urban Development, or the Civil Service Commission. I picked Forest Service because my cousin worked for the Department of Agriculture, which manages the Forest Service. I never meant for it to be a career; it was just a job, a way for us to support our family. I wasn't ever planning to stay. It was just a good government job that paid well and that I needed while attending night school to become a reporter. That was my real goal. It was

very obvious to me in those early days that only men reached the management level at Forest Service. You would see them in a room or around
a table, and they were all white. They were all white men, and I knew
they were making decisions about how to manage people and places I
had never seen.

I don't remember the word Willie James and I argued about, but I
know I looked it up as soon as I got to work. I was right. Willie James was
wrong. My day looked better. After work, I headed back down to Willie
James's job site so we could catch the bus together to pick up the kids. As
I ambled past some of the capital's icons, I admired the green lawns and
saw four of the eighteen national museums on the Mall. I reflected on
how close USFS was to the White House and other tourist attractions.
I should bring the kids down to the Air and Space Museum this weekend,
I thought. I kept going and passed the National Post Office and other
government buildings with their great classic architecture, just like any
other day. As I neared Willie James's job site to meet and take the bus
home, I was startled out of my internal stupor by the sound of traffic, car
horns, and people talking and walking or running for buses, all trying to
get home from a long day's work.

Our babysitter was Ellen, the wife of Lee, who was one—in a group
of six—of Willie James's North Carolina childhood friends. These guys
all came to DC together in the 1960s seeking work. They married, had
families, and socialized together regularly. When we arrived to pick up
the kids, Willie James told Lee about our morning. He was upset that I
would have to miss my first class of the semester that evening because
we couldn't find the car keys. My getting to school was more important
to my husband than it was to me. I knew I could make the class up next
week. Lee said not to worry; Willie James could take his car and bring
it back tomorrow. So, even though I usually drove myself, Willie James
dropped me off that night at the University of Maryland, College Park,
a scenic campus with the eastern university look of red brick and white
columns. The university hosts thousands of trees on a four-hundred-
acre urban forest in the midst of a huge campus, the kind of place a
Forest Service employee pays attention to. It is like a beautiful park, even
in the rain.

We were caught in one of the worst storms in a long time, a torrent
that came down in sheets that cooled the air and chilled you to the bone.

To make matters worse, the professor let us out early, and I did not have a car. I went to the public phone booth in Russell Hall to call Willie James, but the kids answered and said that their dad had already left. He was coming to pick me up early. I thought, *Isn't that just like Willie James?*

I told the kids, "Say your prayers and go to bed. We will be home soon." When I came back to the vestibule, there he sat. Willie James knew I'd had a bad day, and he didn't want me to have to wait. That's how he took care of me. *My thoughtful, sweet husband.* The car was double-parked right outside the hall, but the rain came down so hard we still got soaked as we ran to it.

The University of Maryland's 1,250-acre campus had several exits, and instead of leaving by a direct route, Willie James went "around Dick's barn," taking the long way out of campus, which added fifteen minutes of driving. I still have no idea why he did that, but life would have been entirely different had we taken the regular straight route. I remember asking him, "Why are you going this way?"

"Are you paying attention?" he asked.

"No."

"Honey," he said, "You should always pay attention to where you are, in case you ever have to come back by yourself."

"Fine," I told him, "but I'm with you. I don't need to pay attention because you always know which way to go."

He said it again, "Honey, you should always pay attention to where you are, in case you have to come back by yourself." Then Willie James drove from the campus out onto to the main highway in College Park, Maryland.

We were still talking as the car pulled up to the first stoplight. "Okay, I'll start paying attention," I told him. "And by the way, the word you were going over with Catrina this morning is actually spelled—"

At that moment, there was a loud crash, steel on steel, a grinding noise. My head flew forward and time slowed. I knew I had to look up, to move my heavy head, but it was hard. Finally, I looked over at Willie James, and my entire body shivered. His head lay against the steering wheel. He had passed out, and I had no idea how badly he was hurt. I trembled. I didn't know it at that moment, but my world had changed forever. Suddenly, people were opening my door. They had umbrellas. They were talking, asking me how I was. "I'm fine," I said, "but someone needs to see about my husband." My head throbbed and I could hear sirens. I remembered Leland Hospital was only six blocks away. *They got to us fast. Everything will be okay,* I thought.

Home alone. That's all I could think about. *The kids are home alone and this is going to take some time.* I called my mom. "Mom, there's been an accident and the kids are home alone. Will you pick them up and take them to your house? Willie James and I will be there after we get out of here." I hung up quickly without mentioning the drunk driver down the hall, the same one who ran into us and three other cars before he crashed into a tree. I wondered, *Why am I in this room all by myself? Where is everybody?* I went into the hall but came right back. I could hear the drunk driver singing "99 Bottles of Beer on the Wall." *He better hope Willie James don't find out who he is or his ass is grass,* I thought. *He doesn't know my Willie James!*

I heard the bells and whistles of a trauma cart and my body trembled again. I thought to myself, *There is some kind of emergency out there, no reason for me to check out the commotion.* I figured this was probably why the doctor could not get away to tell me when Willie James and I could go home. I began to walk out the door to check, just as the doctor came in. *It's about time!* In retrospect, it seemed time stopped again. I never got his name. He said, "Mrs. Brown?" I nodded, yes. He said, "Gloria Brown?"

I said, "Yes I'm Gloria Brown."

He said, "Are you alone?"

"Yes."

He shook his head, "I'm so, so sorry." He probably said more, but suddenly I understood, and I fell, unconscious, to the floor.

When I woke up people were all around: my daddy, my aunt and uncle, Willie James's aunt and uncle, and the doctor all hovered over me. At first, I didn't understand. Daddy said the kids were with Mom and they were fine. He was here to take me home. I thought, *Me? Home? Me, home without Willie James?* "How can I go home without Willie James?" I said.

"Baby, Willie James is gone, he's dead," said Daddy.

"No, no!" I cried. "Where is he? I want to see my husband!" The doctor took my hand and led me to the room where Willie James was lying, broken glass still on his face. I tried to clean it off. He seemed to sleep peacefully, and I quietly bled tears as my daddy led me away.

I was thirty years old and suddenly a widow with three children: two girls, ages twelve and eleven, and one son, age nine. *Now what? What do I do? Where do I go? How do I go on? Why go on?* My forty-year-old husband was dead, and I had no clue what to do. Willie James took care of the money. He paid all the bills, rent, insurance, groceries. Both our names were on the checking account, but he earned the big family paycheck. As I'd headed toward my thirtieth birthday on May 7, 1981, I'd had a premonition, a foreboding, as though awaiting the perfect storm, but there was nothing perfect about the squall that hit that night. Everything was wrong. We lost our keys. Rain came down in buckets. It took an extra fifteen minutes to get out of the campus. The light turned red at the wrong time. One small change and my husband would have lived. The only thing perfect was the tempest of destruction that hit our family that night. My life was destroyed. That gloomy year ended for me on September 17, 1981. I was a GS-6 in the Forest Service national office, a rank just above the national average for women and nearly three grades below that of men service-wide.[2]

What a difference a day made. I felt like I never wanted to see another dawn.

My Origins

When I returned to work after Willie James died, I still asked the public, "May I help you?" But the words seemed empty. I was the one who needed help. I guess life-changing events happen all the time. My first big change came at age seven. My mom and dad were great parents, and I was their only child, their firstborn. I came into the world at DC General Hospital, just across the bridge from Alexandria, Virginia, where we lived, not too far from the docks that ran along the Potomac River. I was a happy, smart child, with two proud parents delighting in everything I did.

My early years were filled with good memories. After work in the summertime, Mommy and Daddy would pick me up from the babysitter and we would walk to the docks. I can picture myself then, a plump, round-faced, dark-brown girl, with curly, nappy hair that Mom plaited into big braids. My 6-foot-7-inch dad would put me up on his shoulders, and I felt like I was on top of the world. I always hoped we would end up at the Tastee-Freez, where I would get a vanilla chocolate swirl ice cream cone. Sometimes Dad would pretend to pass right by Tastee-Freez, and I would kick my little feet and slap his gigantic head with my chubby hands. Daddy would stop, turn, and grin: "Ice cream for my two favorite girls?" We were close. We were happy.

My parents, Ruby Baldwin and Harry Foster, met after World War II. I can picture them from photographs: a typical young African American couple, Mom shy and light-skinned, her demeanor reflecting the gentility of the South, Dad a northerner with chocolate brown skin standing confidently in his military uniform. Dad had been a supplies clerk in the US Army Quartermaster Department, a job that led him to work for the General Services Administration after the war. Mom and her three sisters had left home as part of the post–World War II wave of the Second Great Migration, during which millions of African Americans sought jobs, education, and better lives in the North. The young women moved to Virginia, where Mom cleaned houses as she worked on her LPN (licensed practical nurse) degree. When the sisters wanted some fun, they dressed up and went dancing at the Quantico Noncommissioned Officer's Club, where my parents met.

The two of them dated for a while, but when my mother had trouble finding work, she decided to return to Georgia. Dad had a steady job, and he knew how to spend money, so when they were dating, instead of going out she would ask him to just give her the money to put away for him. The story they told is that, while getting ready to leave, my mother gave my father his passbook savings; he looked at it and said there was no way she was going back to my grandmother's! This girl had to be his wife—he couldn't let go of a woman who could save up money like that! And they did very well together. They did so well, in fact, that when I was six years old, they decided to have another baby and moved us away from the river, to 5104 Third Street NW in Washington, DC. And I hated it.

It was a better house and a better neighborhood, but there were no more trips to Tastee-Freez. They also sent for my mother's daughter, the baby she'd had before moving to DC to learn nursing, the sister who was three years older than me. JoAnn had lived with my grandmother in Georgia, but she was not alone. Four other cousins from the other three daughters also lived there. Grandma and Grandpa were sharecroppers. Granddaddy worked in other people's fields, and my grandmother worked in white people's homes cleaning and ironing, and sometimes cooking.

All the girls had left their children with Grandma when they went north, and they sent money to her. It had been a family decision.

We visited my grandparents every summer, but I never liked it. It was the Jim Crow South in the 1950s and the rules were clear, ugly, and demoralizing. Grandma lived on the south side of town, in the Blacks-only neighborhood where the streets were made of dirt, and dust covered everything. The homes there stood on wooden stilts, with just enough space between the bare earth and the house for me to chase chickens underneath. It was different on the other side of town. I realized this as a child when Grandma took me to visit Miss Adelaide, where the white people lived. I saw and felt the centuries-old, southern division between Blacks and Whites that day. Two-to-three-story brick houses lined both sides of the paved road, and white columns marked formal entryways. Grandma wanted to introduce me to Miss Adelaide. "This is my grand-daughter from the North," she told her. "She's really smart because they have good schools up there. Say something to Miss Adelaide, Gloria," my grandmomma said. "Recite that poem you memorized." And I did, feeling sick inside the whole time. I still remember Grandma's tone, deferential and meek, nothing like the strong, proud woman I knew. And there stood Miss Adelaide, commanding and condescending, calling me "a cute little pickaninny" from the North. My grandmomma was pleased that I made Miss Adelaide happy. I wanted to run and hide.

I knew even then that the South wasn't for me! I detested the manda-tory Bible school demanded by Grandma, and I loathed picking cotton on Uncle Leroy's farm, where unending rows of bushes twice my size held pods of cotton, the sticky white fibers clinging to my fingers as I plucked and the pods pricking me. I couldn't pick as much cotton as my cousins, so they always made more money than I did, and I hated them for it. Worse yet, my cousins and sister teased me for being a city girl. I'm sure they knew that I saw them as "country," and not very smart.

I *knew* I was smart. I loved to read and write and planned for a different kind of future. But I was not happy with my life, and I could only blame my once-wonderful parents. We'd had a perfect little fam-ily, so good together, and then along came the others. My mom and dad had turned all their attention to my fat big sister, JoAnn, and my very light-skinned straight-haired baby sister, Lisa. I was dark like my dad. In the African American community, skin tone matters. It mattered on television. It mattered in school. It mattered in daily life. Light-skinned Blacks faced less racism than those of us with darker skin, even from each other. Many darker-skinned people also thought light-skinned people were better looking, and more desirable, capable, and worthwhile. I was just a little girl, so I didn't know how to say this, but I did know that skin color counted. I would tell Dad, "Lisa's not ours, she doesn't look like us." But he adored Lisa and wanted to make sure JoAnn felt loved. It seemed like the only time they paid me attention anymore was when I did something wrong.

A Troubled Past

I first started getting into trouble when Lisa was about three months old. Mommy and Daddy were having one of their monthly dinner parties in our new house. The music was going, people were dancing. I could see them laughing and swaying, Mom with her shoulder-length hair, nicely straightened and pulled into a neat ponytail, Dad tall and handsome. Mom had grown up wearing burlap-sack dresses, but in the North, she and Dad dressed like white people. My parents and their friends took great pride in their dress and style, even for a house party. That night, the men wore trousers and dress shirts, the women blouses and skirts, their crinkled slips flaring as they twirled. Someone was singing along with the Supremes, a song about a lover who left behind a lot of memories.[3] So, when Lisa started crying, I tried to stop her.

I wrapped Lisa in her blankie, went downstairs to the kitchen, and put her in the oven because I remembered Mom saying we had to be quiet when her cakes were in there. Then I called my dad in to show him how I had saved the party. My parents and their guests were horrified. Everyone agreed that I had done a very bad thing, but I knew better. I could have reached the buttons to turn the oven on if I had gotten on my special chair. I wasn't trying to hurt her, just shut her up. The bad news was that my baby sister got me into trouble. The good news was that I got my parents undivided attention for days.

The year after Lisa's birth, my mom began delivering more children, three sons in eighteen-month increments each: Michael, Anthony, and Larry. Michael was cute and light-skinned with good hair, just like Lisa. Anthony, who came next, looked like me and Daddy. So did the last brother, Larry. Mom and Dad took lots of pictures of them. A picture of me is much harder to find. With every baby that arrived, I felt more and more like Mom and Dad ignored me. Before long, I upped the ante to get a response. When I was nine, I stole a bunch of lunches from my fourth-grade schoolmates and threw them in the trash. When the teacher asked me why I'd done it, I said I was hungry, that Mommy and Daddy didn't always feed me. That day, the principal called my parents in to talk. When he explained that they might qualify for food programs, I thought my mother's head would explode. She told the principal, "Gloria Dean lives in a beautiful brick house on Third and Gallatin! We both have good jobs! Why in God's name would we need information on food programs or public assistance?"

That's when I got my first beating from Mom. Dad never beat me, but also never tried to stop her. As I grew older, I continued doing bad things to get my parents' attention, and it worked. Mom responded with angry reprimands and leather belt beatings that left welts on my back and legs. I became convinced I was a bad person. By age twelve, I started running away. I don't remember why that first time, but I knew I would get a beating, so I left. As a teenager, I met Lucy, whose mother was an alcoholic, but very nice to me. Miss Amy didn't care that the kids came to her house, danced, hung out, and slept there. We thought she was a good mother because her household felt free. She fed us, didn't holler, didn't beat people, and she didn't judge. I ran away about fifteen times, always to Lucy's house. My parents never knew where I was.

Even though I was in trouble most of the time and disliked school, I still loved to read and to learn. In fact, I visited the public library two miles from my house every chance I got. I went there to escape, to make up my own perfect world. It was my haven; that is, until one day when I stayed long past my twilight curfew. I remember rushing out the door on the wrong side of the library and thinking, *Okay, you gotta get home, you gotta get home!* I worried that it was dark, but didn't even consider the vulgar, ugly scene that would soon unfold. I simply didn't want to be in trouble with Mommy and Daddy. Never again would I have such innocent fears. As I trudged across the field, suddenly someone grabbed me from behind, threw me to the ground, and put his hand over my mouth. Three teenage boys held me down, one on each side and another at my feet—that's the one who stole my virginity. I know I fought, but I can't recall if I scratched or punched somebody. I just know that everything moved in slow motion.

The rape ended as quickly as it started. When a car came up on that side of the library, its lights shining, one of them yelled, "We gotta go!" They ran off and left me lying there. All I could think about was pulling up my panties and going back into the world without looking like someone who had just been raped. I went home that night and took a very long bath. Everything hurt, especially "down there." And I never told my parents. I never told anyone about it until many, many years later.

Even after the rape, I loved the library. In fact, I went every day for the following week, instead of school, and read about child abuse and rape. I don't remember the numbers now, but I recall that the statistics were high. I was shocked. I know now that reports of forcible rape in DC increased dramatically in the 1960s, nearly a hundred rapes for every hundred thousand women.[4] I also knew from what I read that most women, including me, did not report. As I read, I realized that I was now a statistic, and I increased all the numbers I found by one. I used a pencil to record the stats. If it was five thousand, I wrote 5,001. Later I realized that pencil could be erased. But the rape was real. I cannot forget it. I should have written in ink.

Being bad took on a whole new meaning. Now I was *really* bad, "damaged" goods. *I shouldn't have been walking alone. I should not have stayed out so late. I should have been more modest. I should have fought harder. I should not have allowed those boys to touch me. People will say it was my own fault.* That's how folks talked about rape in those days. I'd heard them and didn't know what to think. I only knew that I hurt deep down inside, and I could not tell anyone. I also thought I would never have a good life like Mom and Dad. Men only married good girls. I had heard this in church, which we went to every Sunday to supposedly commune with God. Instead, we faced the hypocrisy of the preacher and the congregation. Bad things happened to bad people—that's what the church people said. If you are good and godly, nothing happens. Mom and Dad had even taken me to our pastor to discuss my behavior. I never asked them if they knew that Reverend Taylor would brush his arm across women's breasts as though no one could see him.

I didn't know it then, but what happened gave me the sense that I could come back from anything. I became more daring. I had survived

rape. What could be worse for a child? I knew how to compartmental-
ize, how to move forward with strength, how to keep things to myself. I
became even more willing to challenge my parents and myself. I learned
that even when the worst thing happens to you, you can survive. And, you
can do it by yourself. I figured out how to live the life that I wanted. Rape
is never good. The outcome is always very bad. But I also learned that
fending for myself was more important to me than my virginity. I started
taking a switchblade to the library in case that ever happened again, and
I never stayed till dark.

Finding Home

I decided that something needed to change. I had taken every opportunity to draw attention to myself at school and at home, but always in the
wrong way. My parents were not bad people, just so wrapped up with my
siblings that they did not recognize my pain. Even if they had known, I
thought they would see me as the culprit. So when I turned sixteen in
1967, I got a job at Miles Long Sandwich Shop near Twelfth and H Streets
NE in Washington, DC. And when I saved up enough money, I moved
into my own studio apartment two blocks away. I was in the twelfth grade
when I dropped out of Calvin Coolidge High School and took the GED. I
always told people I had graduated.

I was seventeen when I met Willie James Brown, a twenty-six-year-
old Vietnam veteran. When Willie James came into the shop, we'd talk for
hours. Before long, he started walking me home, telling me about the war
and his "boys," everyday stories about soldiers, rather than the horrors of
war. The young men would trade cigarettes and other goodies that arrived
in their care packages. They all knew the fear that each of them shared,
but nobody showed it. Sometimes I cried at these powerful stories, especially when Willie James talked about the pain of losing men from his
platoon. He also told me you have to go on anyway. You don't get time to
grieve. Little did he know how those words would haunt me, and help me.

Willie James made me happy. He took me to all the places I'd spoken
of while he ate his sandwiches. I was surprised that he remembered my
stories and found ways to recreate the experiences or make new memories. On my days off the two of us played in the city, visiting sites like
the Smithsonian museums and the Lincoln Memorial. Twice we toured

Monticello, Thomas Jefferson's primary plantation. We even went to the Washington Monument and the White House. But our favorite place was the Washington National Zoo and the Ringling Brothers Barnum and Bailey Circus, the last place I remembered being close with my parents before my siblings came along. I had finally found someone I loved and who loved me back—without my being bad: Willie James Brown, the preacher's grandson.

We married at my parents' house and went straight to having a family. Camille (who we call Nicki) and Catrina were only eleven months apart. We waited a couple of years and then we had Andre. "Finally, a son," Willie James said.

"Yes," I said, "and your son convinced me we will not have any more babies." The girls were a little over seven pounds when they were born; Andre was well over nine pounds! Ouch!

Losing Home

Willie James Brown was Mrs. Gloria Brown's bridge over troubled water, a really good dad and involved. We had thirteen years of smooth sailing. Willie James had picked up where Mommy and Daddy stopped. He had taken care of me, and losing him left me as emotionally destroyed at thirty years old as I had been after the rape at age twelve. I was bereft, devastated, living in a daze. I started drinking too much, and every day was a struggle; yet, I continued to work. Nobody knew about my drinking, and I remained the voice of the Forest Service. I took the calls and answered the letters that came in to the national information office. If you needed a more detailed answer, I forwarded the query to the appropriate department or specialist. If you wanted material about Smokey the Bear or Woodsy the Owl for your classroom, I sent it to you. I would make your requests come true.

After Willie James died, I guess you could say that the Forest Service became my family and support system, but not right away. First, I had to let go of Willie James. We never did go back to our house. The night of the accident, we went straight to my mom's and stayed for a couple of months. Then we moved to a three-bedroom apartment, with enough space for Andre and me to each have our own rooms and for the girls to share the master, but you could hear people going back and forth, elevators running up and down day and night. Our home had been in a middle-class neighborhood. The apartment was a real contrast; people hanging out, break-ins, people without jobs—a low-income neighborhood, which was all I could afford.

I grieved hard. My family took care of my husband's body and of getting me and the kids to North Carolina. I know Willie James had a military funeral with an honor guard and a volley of rifle shots. I know they folded a flag and gave it to me, and that each of the kids dropped a rose on his casket. That's all I remember. I was physically present, but mentally vacant. That state of mind continued for a long time. The pain was so wretched that I would come home, get a drink, take my prescription drugs, pore over a box of pictures of him and the family, and wait. I clung to that box of pictures as though I could will him back through his image. Every night I put the kids to bed and sat in the living room in agony and hope, waiting for the drugs to numb the pain as I anticipated Willie James's return. I could not, would not let him go. I even took the box of pictures to work with me every day. And then one day, somehow, I left the picture box on the train. I was devastated. I called Metro every day and returned to that train daily for several weeks, but they never showed up. Losing those pictures was like having Willie James taken all over again, this time for good. But somehow that loss disconnected me from my husband and sent me a message: Get your act together. Get on with life, if not for yourself, for his kids.

Strategizing the Future

That's when I began to see the Forest Service as my salvation. I didn't know a lot about the Forest Service from the ground up then, except that I worked in the Washington office (WO). Before Willie James died, I had planned to become a television reporter, a choice he supported. Now I could not afford to start at the bottom of print or a live medium and decided, instead, to work myself up through the ranks of the Forest Service. My children had entered the public school system where we lived, which was motivation enough for change: How could I get them out of that school, out of the neighborhood, and into a safe environment, conducive to learning and living? I decided to become a survivor, not a victim. First goal, finish my degree in journalism. Next, figure out how to get from A to B to C in an organization that had been predominantly white and male for three-quarters of a century.

While I finished my degree at night, during the day I worked for Bill Hamilton, who was under the director of information, Bob Lake. Across the hall was the Resources Planning Act (RPA) assessment office, directed by Lamar Beasley, a forester by training, an administrator by talent. RPA dealt with planning, assessing, and implementing environmental laws, areas that became more and more important in the 1970s and 1980s. Lamar came into my office now and then to get information and publications; while there he'd talk to me in his smooth, calm southern drawl about family, the day, and agency issues. No one engaged me like Lamar, though other directors visited with me too: Wendell Jones, director of timber management; Mike Barton, director of watershed and soils; the Fish and Wildlife director; and the recreation director, Lyle Laverty, to name a few. For them, the conversation was light chatter while waiting for materials. For me, it provided opportunity to understand the agency and what happened in the "field." I didn't stop learning after a few conversations. I listened harder and became more determined to advance. When I didn't have evening classes, I volunteered to staff the chief's office after his secretary went home. It was not unusual for Chief Max Peterson and Associate Chief Dale Robertson to stay late for meetings with members of Congress or the public. This gave me the opportunity to greet those individuals and dignitaries. I took their coats, made them drinks, and kept on smiling even though I made barely enough money to feed my kids. In the midst of the pleasantries, I strategized about how to move up.

I'm sure I was invisible to the chief and deputy chief, and to directors and members from Congress. But if the chief left his door open, I eavesdropped. I listened and I learned. I met leading political figures from Oregon, like Senator Mark Hatfield and Congressman Peter DeFazio, who talked about the far-off Pacific Northwest and its timber. This was the 1980s, and the Northwest and Alaska remained frontrunners in an emerging crisis over old-growth forests, the spotted owl, the marbled murrelet, and other natural resource debates. How could there be a balance between environment and economy? How could the Forest Service achieve its multiple-use mission, while contending with environmental mandates? Congress expected the Forest Service to support itself. Northwest communities expected jobs. That meant high timber harvests. Scientists and environmentalists expected the Forest Service to adhere to environmental laws and to protect habitat. That meant reducing timber harvests. The agency was being sued left and right. Some Northwest protesters even chained themselves to or placed spikes in old-growth trees to prevent loggers from cutting them down. A woman named Julia Butterfly Hill lived for two years in one of Northern California's ancient redwoods to effectively stop harvests. It was a rough period for the Forest Service.

At the time, the Department of Agriculture took a hands-off approach. The chief handled our business in Washington and in the field, with a clear line through the regional foresters to national forest supervisors and district rangers. While the WO made policy, employees worked "on the ground" and "in the field," cruising timber, managing sales, clearing trails, cutting hazardous trees, fighting fire, and writing environmental assessments (EAs) for fish and wildlife projects. If you worked in Washington, and paid attention, you learned about who was who, agency problems, and how politics worked. If you wanted to move up in the Forest Service hierarchy, you had to know how DC operated and who had the power. If you were not interested, you just did your job.

I had just done my job until Willie James died. Now, as I tried to figure out how to enter the Forest Service chain of command, I assessed my performance. I was good at my job and could answer nearly any question or address any issue posed by the public, whether on the telephone or in the chief's office. I interacted as comfortably with national figures as I did with employees in the basement. I knew how to take initiative and get things done. I also knew that I needed champions if I wanted to move up.

One high-level administrator who stood out for me was Lamar Beasley. He was different. When Lamar spoke, he talked *to* me, not at me. I watched how Lamar treated his employees and liked what I saw. He was kind, respectful, and made time for conversations. I also noticed that the individuals who worked in his department on short-term details typically served for three to six months and were then promoted out of the Washington office. I began to see that Lamar created a breeding ground for future rangers, regional office staff, and others developing their careers. Departments like timber and recreation also produced rangers, but more advancement seemed to come through Lamar's RPA office than through any other. So, one day I asked, "Lamar, I see people coming through your office and getting promoted to offices in the field. How can I come work for you?"

Lamar flashed his million-dollar smile and said, "That's easy Gloria. The next position you qualify for, just apply."

And that is exactly what I did. The next position that came available was secretary for RPA. No one understood why I would leave I&E to take a job as a secretary when I had a degree in journalism. But I didn't see movement in I&E like I saw in RPA. You know the saying, "the best laid plans often go awry"? Well, I got the job, but the same week I started, Lamar was promoted to deputy chief for legislative affairs. I remember wondering, *Now what do I do?* I would not give up! *My plan to advance should still work, but I need new supporters*, I thought. I quickly targeted my bosses, the new director of RPA, Tom Hamilton, and assistant RPA director John Butruille. Little did I know that this relationship would matter even more later on. Meanwhile, when I started asking questions about how to advance, Tom and John made it clear that the best way would be to leave the Washington office.

Meeting My Destiny

I needed to understand how a region works "in the field." So, Tom and John facilitated a two-week detail to the information office in Region 6, in Oregon, on the other side of the country. This was my first plane ride ever, and it exposed me to an entirely new world. As the plane circled to land at the Portland International Airport, I was struck by the brilliant white-topped peaks of Mount Hood. I had seen the Smoky Mountains, but never anything like this! I also quickly realized that Oregon's population was as white as the mountain's peaks. I had worked with Caucasians for a long time, but never before had I seen a place with no African Americans. Yes, I learned there were a few in the state—about 37,000 in a population of 2.5 million—but they were not very visible in the Portland Regional Office (RO), the city's downtown area, and especially not on the Forest Service districts I visited.[5] The most diversity I saw in Portland was in the personnel office, the mailroom, and the civil rights office; when I visited the Willamette National Forest, I saw no people of color. There were women, but at the forest and district levels, no one looked like me.

What I did see everywhere I looked was Northwest green, the color of money in the Forest Service, and the hue of deliverance for me. Oregon's lush Willamette Valley took my breath away as an employee named Jerry Mason drove me to the Willamette National Forest supervisor's office in Eugene. The Willamette National Forest stretches more than a hundred miles along the western slope of the Cascade Range, extending from Mount Jefferson east of Salem to the Calapooya Mountains northeast of Roseburg. Mount Hood dominates the Portland landscape, while Mount Jefferson looms above the crystal-clear lakes, cascading waterfalls, and vibrant plant life of the Willamette Valley and its national forest. To me, these were some of the prettiest landscapes in the country. Of course, I hadn't seen a lot. Although I had been with the Forest Service for nearly ten years, I had never been in a national forest.

When I saw the massive trees, bigger than any living thing I had ever seen, soaring hundreds of feet into the air, a million fragrant needles sending oxygen into the atmosphere, I felt that I was in a cathedral, a church more powerful than any other. The Douglas-firs, true firs, and pines towered over me. Brilliant shades of green and gold moss and lichen brought the forest to life, while the flaming red of Indian fireweed burned into my consciousness, and the solitude of the trails calmed my soul. There were no cars, no streetlights, and very few people; just trees, rivers, and wildlife. I had never known solitude like that, even in a park. At a cookout in DC, there were people everywhere. This was different. People walked the trails, but the forest enclosed you in solitude. I had sent out pamphlets about forest ecology but had never walked in the forest. I had provided schools with educational materials about the environment, but had never seen old growth. For me, visiting the Willamette forest was like going into a darkroom and having the light come on slowly to reveal a new world. I had so many firsts, my parents didn't believe my stories. I decided then to one day work on the Willamette. Daddy did say that if I ever got to live in Oregon, he would love to visit and fish for some salmon. I eventually got to Oregon, but Dad died before he could catch that fish.

I had never eaten salmon before my detail to Oregon. I eat it all the time now. The food was good, the scenery fantastic, and it was the cleanest place I had ever been. The highlight of my trip was a black bear running across Highway 101 near Cape Perpetua. I had never seen a wild animal outside of the National Zoo. That did it. I went home determined to get out of Washington, DC. I also decided that Oregon might be a little too wild and was definitely way too white for us. I hoped to make my next detail to Region 8, Atlanta, Georgia.

When I returned, Tom, John, and I had several meetings about my long-term goals. I wanted to eventually be a forest information officer, and someday direct one of our nine regional information offices. Later, I realized what I really wanted was to be one of the decision makers, a line officer. In the meantime, Tom, John and I decided the first step was to change my position series. Each job title came with a number, a pay scale, and a particular fit in the agency. And only foresters—not secretaries—could become line officers. Because of my journalism degree, the agency could classify me as a 1035 Information Specialist, a move away from the clerical (318) category I'd had for nearly a decade, the classification of most women in the WO Forest Service. I applied for an RPA Information Specialist (GS-1035-7). As an information specialist I could work with detailers who came to the WO to get their tickets stamped while working on the national RPA program, then engaged in evaluating the nation's forests. My duties included some writing, proofreading, and editing, a step up from secretarial work and a great way to learn about national issues and meet important individuals. I got to work with people like Beth Horn (later director of information, R-1) and many others who became agency leaders—district rangers, forest supervisors, and regional directors. Some became my supporters, mentors, and advisers.

By 1986, the time had come for me to depart the WO, where I had worked for more than a decade—to leave my family, friends, and the church I had stopped attending. I had spent the previous three years gaining the knowledge and skills to advance in the agency. Tom and John agreed that I was ready and started making calls to get me a job in one of the nine regional offices of the Forest Service. I thought I would be most comfortable in the South. Region 8 could provide new friends, a new church, and a new beginning for me and the kids. But I was only a GS-7, so when Beth Horn answered the call with a GS-9/11 public affairs position in her information office, I applied. I got the job—in Missoula, Montana, a state with more mountains, more forests, and more white people than most places in the country.

CHAPTER 2

Mother Bear Meets Smokey: Heading West

IT MIGHT SEEM CRAZY FOR A SINGLE, thirty-eight-year-old African American woman to leave everything she's ever known to move from Washington, DC, to Missoula, Montana, with a state population less than 1 percent Black. That statistic alone should have made me pause. It would be tremendously strange for all of us, after a lifetime in the DC area, but I knew I was professionally stuck in the Washington office. It could take decades for me to advance, and I needed to support my family *now*. Leaving the area five years after my husband's death was hard. My children were in high school by then, and I realized I had taken my family for granted. In fact, I had a whole lifetime taken for granted. As I pondered the move, a sense of overwhelming grief struck me. But I had to go.

I had always been a big city girl—never thought about the other side of the country, except to send out brochures to people interested in national forests. That said, improving my career meant risking everything for the unknown. I remember thinking, *What if I'm not successful? What will I do? Where will I go?* But I was about to take the most important road trip of my life. I had no time to fret. A friend had provided my only previous connection to Montana, a book titled *A River Runs Through It* by Norman Maclean. The book was about two brothers growing up in Missoula, Montana, one of whom worked for the Forest Service. Their lives seemed inviting, serene, and bucolic. Norman, the story's main character, learns about taking supplies into the high country from old Bill, a Forest Service packer. Norman explains that the mules seemed to know exactly what to do. They worked in unison, placid and purposeful: "The moment the outfit was on the road each [mule] assumed his own character and collectively all became Bill's string, Bill's outfit—Bill himself, his favorite saddle horse, his favorite pack horse, and his dog—were about the finest the early Forest Service had to offer."[1] I had wondered if I would ever get to do something like that.

Norman talked about Missoula the way I would talk about growing up in Washington, DC, as familiar with nature as I with the city. The book serenely depicts the 1930s, but I grew up in the 1960s—with the civil rights movement, inner city violence, African American migration from the South, and the Vietnam War. My life experience had been far from tranquil. Where the book discussed wide-open spaces, I thought about monuments, museums, businesses, and row houses. The character saw brilliant stars and a huge moon nightly. I often saw the moon, but very few stars. His rivers were different from DC's Anacostia or the Chesapeake Bay. His had fish and fowl. Mine had trash.

Road Trip West

I knew that life would be different in Missoula. I would be leaving behind important relationships and making new ones. I had been dating John Whitlow, the national director of Big Brothers of America for a while then. I met John when Andre went on a very long wait-list for a big brother. John helped match Andre with an outstanding, professional big brother, who provided a good male role model. If I stayed in DC with John, I could take a different path, but I had decided to advance in my career. Instead of marriage and everything that went with it, I asked my boyfriend to help me move to Montana. As we set out, I thought of John, my son, and I as three African American pioneers going west. But Andre and I would stay; John would return to the city.

As we started our journey on the I-495 Beltway toward Maryland, Andre and I were most impressed by the stark appearance of the majestic Appalachian Mountains. I used this opportunity to share some history with my son. I told him about my family trips south to see my grandmother. We had traveled at night, with Mom and Dad taking turns driving, so we could get to Georgia as soon as possible. We never stopped at restaurants or hotels. My mom always brought great food—fried chicken, ham, fruit snacks, and chocolate cake—and a bucket for us to use the bathroom. We ate, slept, and peed in the car. My dad was afraid of being stopped by the police. He knew that a black man had as good a chance of getting hung as getting a ticket. Those were the logistics of traveling south as an African American in the 1950s and 1960s. I explained how Georgia boldly and proudly flew the Confederate flag, and that things were different there. Ice cream parlors and water fountains carried labels like "colored" or "White Only," and we had to be careful which we used. Just twenty years earlier, we still had to go in the back door of the movie house and sit in the balcony. I told my son that when we traveled north to see relatives, the trip had been different, more tranquil. We didn't have to drive at night or sleep and eat in the car, but Dad still worried about being stopped by the police.

Much had changed since then. Much had not. I wanted him to grow up with positive memories of road trips, without fear and tension. Without going to the bathroom in the car. Racial tension between Whites and Blacks still existed, only now the racism lay under the surface. As we moved west, we saw a far whiter America than I'd ever seen before. I remember asking John if we should travel at night. He said we didn't need to worry about safety, not now. I was not convinced. My only experience with the West, aside from my trip to Portland, had been unsettling. I'd been on a Forest Service detail in St. Anthony, Idaho, where people literally stared at me as I bicycled through town and kept staring after their red lights turned green. My very presence had stopped traffic. The farther west I went without the safety blanket of the Washington office of the Forest Service, the more goosebumps I got.

We traveled on Highway 80 and passed Hagerstown, the last metropolis in Maryland, then jogged around the State of Pennsylvania to its western turnpike. I had been in the South, in the East, and in the West, but the landscape in between surprised me. Miles and miles of open country and shamrock-green fields spiraled before us. That is when I recognized the main theme of my first road trip to the West—the major differences between places and people in this nation. When we stopped for snacks at a 7-Eleven in Pennsylvania, or got gas, I noticed that people wore overalls and t-shirts. I had never seen clothing like this, except on television's *Green Acres*. They sounded different, too, spoke more slowly and called Coca-Cola "pop" instead of soda.

The trip juxtaposed rural and urban as we rapidly transitioned from place to place. A few miles north, the iconic City of Pittsburgh rose above the skyline, diverging from the rural setting that had enveloped us just moments before. John had mapped the journey, so we knew where to go for food and sleep. Still, it felt odd when we ate at a Howard Johnson's and slept at a Motel 6, where there were no black people and everyone stared. The next morning the highway took us toward the Ohio border, where only cornfields, orchards, massive vegetable gardens, and farmhouses broke up the tidy rural countryside, in stark contrast to industrial Pennsylvania and unlike the flat plains we soon entered. Just when I thought I'd hit the eastern edge of America, the landscape flowed easily from open spaces to urban places, with the cities of Springfield and greater Dayton, Ohio, sprawled in front of us for miles. We headed for Indiana and passed the beautiful town of Richmond before the scene again transitioned to small communities and farmscapes.

Our journey on Interstate 70 ended as we left behind this seemingly subdued city, a midland American town painted gray by the dust of steel mills. Chicago felt more familiar, with back-to-back traffic, big houses, office buildings that provided jobs to swarms of people from the inner city, and black people. The suburbs seemed to go on forever, until we reached Joliet and returned to Midwest rural sights and small towns. A few hours later we came to the massive Mississippi River at the Illinois-Iowa state line. Summertime Iowa cemented stereotypes I had about the state, the miles and miles of cornfields, farmhouses, and a landscape that repeated all the way to the Nebraska border. At the Council Bluffs/Omaha bridge, we caught sight of the great Missouri River, dark and muddy like the Mississippi. Eastern Nebraska resembled Iowa, and as we traveled the last two-thirds of the state, we drove along the Platte River.

We soon left the quivering lowland aspens along the Platte and started climbing gradually toward the great Rocky Mountains. There, gravel and rock held together huge boulders, while nature showered these rocks with intermittent flows of water. We left the Platte north of the Colorado state line and drove toward the mountains of Wyoming, moving from Cheyenne to Rawlings, where we turned north. High mountain passes and rocky ravines greeted us as we passed through the Grand Tetons toward Yellowstone National Park. Now I understood why this majestic place was the cornerstone of the National Park System. We excitedly took pictures all the way through the park, surprised to see snow in July, along with moose and elk. We patiently waited with other tourists (the most diversity I'd seen since I'd left DC) to see Old Faithful spurt at its designated time.

A Whole New World

As we headed into Missoula, my emotions shifted from fear to joy to excitement. Then I remembered that Forest Service personnel were predominantly Caucasian and male, with Missoula a nearly all-white city. I started having bad thoughts. Did Missoula have Ku Klux Klan? What about the Aryan Nations? I knew they had settled on a compound in nearby Idaho in the 1970s. I also knew that their brand of Christian identity meant hate, not love, with anti-Semitism and a brand of white nationalism lying just below the surface. Thank God there was no internet then, or I might have learned of the many klaverns of the Montana KKK in the 1920s and decided against going. Had I realized how deeply embedded these groups were, how much hate could easily surround me in Montana, I'd have been scared to death. I was a single African American mother taking my three black children into an all-white world.

Even as I fretted, I knew I had to change my mind-set, to maintain the positive outlook that had always sustained me. I had been surrounded by mostly decent and good white people in the national office, and I didn't think they would send me somewhere dangerous. We couldn't stay in Missoula with me thinking negatively. I reminded myself that I had left my parents to join a bigger family; at least that's how most Caucasians viewed the Forest Service—as a family. Since the turn of the century, wives and children had accompanied hardy rangers to remote forested outposts, where the women (always white) often provided two-for-one services. They lived with their husbands at fire lookouts in the summer and staffed guard houses and ranger offices or prepared correspondence and answered phones the remainder of the year.[2] These Forest Service wives had been unpaid social directors, cooking, cleaning, and organizing compounds that were both home and work, places where men chopped wood for the winter and children played ball and rode bicycles, while rangers negotiated with loggers and organized work crews for thinning stands of timber. Like military wives sent west, these women banded together, even creating a Forest Service Wives Club that lasted into the 1980s.

As the agency expanded numerically in that decade, it added more than ten thousand permanent full-time employees,[3] bringing many other women and people of color into the Forest Service fold. I was part of the old and new Forest Service, part of the demographic change. I had been with the agency for more than a decade, and I believed in the Forest Service I'd known in the DC office. I told myself, *There is no need to worry about bigots or discrimination because of the color of my skin.* I soon learned the reality, though, that many people did respond to me solely based on skin color, and they did the same with my kids. In fact, as we went on a driving tour, just after the girls arrived, a car full of teenagers pulled up next to us at a stoplight and yelled "You're out of place, niggers!" My children knew the history of these words when spoken by white people. Even before they'd arrived, they'd heard horror stories of burning crosses and people being chased out of town with guns. Missoula scared them. But I told the kids, "Okay, so you've had your first contact with racism in Missoula. Let's see where we go from here."[4] Inside, I thought, *Why in God's name did we come here?*

But I knew the answer. I came from the Washington office (WO) to the regional office (RO)—which was not considered "the field"—for the experience. Organizational structure and information on policies and issues descended uniformly from the WO to each regional office. The agency has nine regional offices (no Region 7) and eight forestry and forest products research stations in the United States. These regions include several national forests, each with a forest supervisor's office. Each forest has several ranger districts, with hundreds nationwide. The issues and landscapes differ among regions, but they all follow the same rules, and I was headed in the right direction, getting to know every level of the Forest Service. Beth Horn, whom I met during her detail to the WO, would now be my boss. She also became one of the first to support my long-term advancement goals and to provide the professional training I needed. After a year of performance and training in Missoula, I would receive a promotion to GS-11, a status that cemented my professional level in the agency. It also meant more money.

Training on the Ground: Wilderness and Fire

My early training in Montana brought me face-to-face with the land itself. Wilderness training included packing a mule for backcountry trails. I had to take notes, because we had a test later, but thank God I didn't have to pack that mule! The Forest Service hired an "outfitter," an old-timer named Bucky, for a two-day trip into the Bob Marshall Wilderness. Bucky was straight out of the Old West, just what I expected: a short, skinny, bow-legged guy with baggy pants, but with a seemingly home-made bowler hat rather than cowboy gear. He had a huge horse and a string of mules, each with its own name. Bucky loaded their backs with food, camp stoves, cookware, blankets, and all of our gear. I was thrilled to find that we ate well in the woods. Bucky grilled steaks over an open fire, while beans bubbled on the camp stove. Biscuits and huckleberry cobbler, made from the sweet special berry found only in damp forests of the Pacific Northwest, topped off our meal. It was as good or better than what I'd have at home.

I found myself surrounded by people who had worked half their lives in the woods, who shared stories about hunting and fishing, activities I had never done. The talk around the fire educated me. I had all the questions: Where did these huckleberries come from? Do we have to worry about bears or mountain lions? What about snakes? I found out there were black bears, but no dangerous snakes. I also learned to identify scat. I had never seen a cow patty, much less grizzly poop. The former is round, crusted over, and flat; the latter resembles dog poo, but bigger. I learned that huckleberries grow abundantly among the redwoods and Douglas-fir. Native people had been picking the berries each summer for thousands of years. Non-Natives had turned harvesting into an enterprise that included wine, candy, and jellies. Now, the little purple berry was at the heart of one of many multiple-use conflicts on national forest lands.

We camped in the Bob Marshall Wilderness, designated in 1964 and the third-largest wilderness complex in the lower forty-eight states, with more than 1.5 million acres.[5] I had never seen anything like the composite of rugged peaks, alpine forests, cascading lakes, meadows, and big river valleys. Trees grew taller than eastern office buildings. Wildflowers looked painted. You could camp only if you carted your garbage in and out, buried your human scat, and left no trace behind. For the Forest Service, wilderness means set-aside areas and maintaining the landscape in its original setting. Cutting timber is not allowed, and motor vehicles are prohibited.

I had never ridden a horse before, had never even touched a pony; yet, here I was learning to mount, ride, and steer a live animal. At first, I was too excited to be afraid. As we clomped down narrow trails over canyons, our guide told me not to worry. Then I realized that if my horse fell over, I would surely die. I'd never thought about dying at work before, but as I looked down from the back of a five-foot-high animal into a ravine ten feet below a trail already hundreds of feet high, it suddenly felt possible. I stopped looking down. This was one experience of many that made me say to myself, *I can do this!*

Learning to function in the outdoors is a process, and doing it in the wilderness is an art. Putting up my tent was so hilarious that I had to laugh at myself. I used a Forest Service tent and tried to set it up by reading the how-to instructions, all the while thinking, *I have no idea what I'm doing! Why would so many people say they like this?* I finally got some help from the guys, and I later grew to love tent camping. Now I can put up a tent in just a few minutes! It turned out that the worst part of this field training was going to the bathroom. I had known there was no toilet, but somehow, I thought there would be a Porta Potty. I was wrong!

I remember that first night by the south fork of the Flathead River. As a child, I was always afraid of the dark, but not in my tent. Before I fell asleep in the black darkness, I thought I heard something rustling outside, but rather than fear I felt the peace of a grandiose nature that I found more soothing than church on Sunday. I had never before awakened to the sounds of a forest or the tranquility that comes with the burble of a flowing river. You see sunlight shining through tent flaps and hear the sounds of birds whistling and leaves blowing through the trees. The serenity of those sounds and sights convinced me I was on the right path. The trip home was far less frightening because I had learned to trust my horse.

The Forest Service takes fire very seriously. I knew that from the WO, but in the field *everyone* had to be trained, even office staff like me. Firefighting training felt like training for the Olympics. We trained three to four hours per day and hiked with two-pound, specially designed fire packs, sweating under our hard hats while putting out fires we had started ourselves. We wore standard Forest Service gear, the agency "pickle-suit": dark-green pants, yellow shirts, and our yellow hard hats marked with the classic Forest Service insignia. For the first time as a Forest Service employee, I had to buy a pair of steel-toed boots designed for working in the woods. I even learned how to build a fire line by digging the real thing!

We used Pulaskis, the firefighting tool created by Ranger Ed Pulaski after the great fires of August 20, 1910, that burned more than three million acres in Washington, Idaho, and Montana. Pulaski's superiors later called him "the hero of the big burn" for his perseverance, rational thinking, and the courage that helped save lives. As fire raged above the town of Wallace, Idaho, seemingly preventing escape, Pulaski tried to deliver supplies to firefighters on the mountainside. When his packers deserted him, he rounded up about fifty men trying to escape the burning hillsides. As the fire thundered toward them, Pulaski took his crew toward a deep mining tunnel a mile away, one he hoped would be large and deep enough to protect them. "Everyone inside the tunnel," he ordered as the men reached the shaft. When some hesitated, "afraid to crawl into a darkened hole of a mountain on fire, Pulaski put his hand on his revolver and repeated: 'Everyone inside, Now!'"[6] One man burned to death outside the mine shaft. Five perished within. Pulaski became disfigured and lost sight in one eye. But he lived to tinker in his blacksmith shop and create what author Timothy Egan claims is "obvious in retrospect," a single-handled tool with an axe on one side and a hoe-type blade on the other. One side cuts wood and the other can scrape out a fire line. Although never compensated for his heroism, or his invention, Pulaski's name and story live on in the minds and hands of every firefighter trained by the Forest Service.[7]

Reading about that 1910 fire solidified my understanding of the need for fire shelter training. A Forest Service fire shelter looks like a cross between a sleeping bag and a human-sized silver bullet. The shelters are made of aluminum foil on the outside, with a silica weave that repels the heat. Timing is everything when it comes to getting into one of these shelters. You lie on the ground, facedown and spread-eagled. Both hands hold the front of the shelter and both feet clamp down the back, as every inch of material is wrapped tightly around your body. Every firefighting team has a leader who decides when to deploy shelters. The fire has to be coming right at you, and you have anywhere from minutes to seconds to take cover. The team captain's main job is to keep people from panicking, because panic means death. Those people are really good.

These first outdoor experiences stand out in my memory because I learned a lot about myself and about the Forest Service. I had mustered the courage to tackle challenges a young single mother from DC could have never imagined—horses, axes, fire, bugs, and peeing in the great outdoors. All of this gave me confidence to face the future. By working at the regional level, I became more intimate with a Forest Service that had long been my acquaintance. When not training, my usual duties included working with staff specialists to prepare briefing books, writing speeches, and facilitating meetings. I assisted in preparing maps for "show-me" trips that introduced out-of-town guests to forest projects and places. I also wrote human-interest stories about employees working in the woods—tree planters laboring after a cut, or a recreation camp opening for the spring and summer.

Another important assignment included working with Senator Max Baucus and his staff to develop a wilderness bill for Montana. Little did I know then that we were in the middle of a decade-long drawn out "civil war over wilderness," one of the biggest in the twentieth century. The Wilderness Act, passed in 1964, sought to retain undeveloped federal land in "its primeval character and influence, without permanent improvements or human habitation." It identified nine million acres of wilderness at the law's inception, land that contrasted with "areas where man and his works dominate the landscape" and recognized places "where the earth and its community of life are untrammeled by man, where man himself is a visitor who does not remain."[8] Montana had been a major player in wilderness preservation, with nearly four million acres of federal land reserved in 1964, another 1.6 million in the 1970s, and the 250,000-acre Lee Metcalf Wilderness in 1983. Our work supported Senator Max Baucus's efforts to create a final wilderness area in a state that many saw as developed enough, while others disliked preventing development.

The staff and I responded to questions from the senator's office about areas he wanted included as wilderness and the parameters for it. I interviewed regional staff specialists to determine the response and acted as liaison to provide them answers. We took their information and placed it into context, which meant figuring out the who, what, where, and why of selection. Then we brought in staffers from DC, who made recommendations about whether or not to include specific locales. Our discussions prevented the Forest Service from identifying areas that neither the senator nor the governor would accept. I felt like a glorified messenger, but this was a level of communication with a legislator I'd never had before. I hadn't realized how much time and work went into the policy proposals that came through the WO for review or approval, and I had been only slightly aware of lobbyists and special interest groups in DC. A lot more goes into the laws governing public lands than most people think. I soon learned that disagreement with the senator's staff would result in silence. Our job was strictly to assist them with their needs, not tell them what we in the field thought about issues. They wanted their inquiries answered, not questions from us. Providing agency opinion and policy was a job left to the chief's office. Still, the many show-and-tell meetings intended to help the public understand proposals impressed me. More striking was our role in gathering together multiple publics and considering their opinions on resource management. I knew that these public meetings stemmed from legal mandates prompted by the National Environmental Policy Act (1969) and the National Forest Management Act (1976), but remained impressed by the process.

I organized, watched, listened, and, later, took my cues from those who seriously considered the needs of people with interests in the land. I was glad Senator Baucus's bill got through Congress. He had tried to reserve wilderness terrain since the early 1980s, with major disputes stemming from the amount of land slated for protection. The public land reservation I had been supporting resulted in a 1987 bill that passed both the State House and Senate, and designated 1.4 million acres as wilderness, with another 800,000 as wilderness recreation or "study" areas for possible later inclusion. Nearly four million acres would then be opened to development, which could mean logging, mining, oil drilling, and other multiple uses like snowmobiling and dirt bikes. Looking back, I found that the bill we worked so hard to help prepare was pocket-vetoed by President Reagan on November 4, 1988, just days before the election. The immediate outcome was no wilderness area and the loss of a Democratic senatorial seat in Montana. I'm glad I didn't know all of that as I carried my positive attitude into the rest of my career.

Workforce Diversity

I came to Montana at the height of efforts to create what top leadership called a "multicultural organization." Between 1978, when the Civil Service Reform Act charged federal agencies with creating a "workforce reflective of the nation's diversity," and 1986, the number of women and people of color in the agency grew. By 1992, the Forest Service had doubled the percentage of female employees to 40 percent and increased minorities from 8 to 15 percent. But the transition to Missoula was stark. Nearly everyone was white—clericals, professionals, supervisors, everybody. *That* was the face of the Forest Service. I realized I hadn't had a correct view of the agency in Washington, DC. Region 1, which includes all of Montana and North Dakota, Northern Idaho, and a small square of South Dakota, had only eleven Blacks in 1987, in a three-thousand-person workforce. Only three of us were women. Other minorities included 125 American Indians, 43 Hispanics, and 23 Asians/Pacific Islanders.[9] The Forest Service was also *extremely* male. That I'd known, though I hadn't experienced it in DC like I did in the field.[10]

There were some benefits to being the only African American woman in the regional office. I was in public affairs, but I immediately went to work on diversity issues in Missoula, and when Jesse Jackson came to town, I got invited to dinner. No one invited me to meet presidential candidates in DC, nor had I been considered the resident expert on race, which I really was not. I could have been offended, but one of the best, most unexpected, and challenging parts of my job was providing diversity training to the field. It turned out that most of my diversity work focused on gender issues, though it included some ethnic and cultural diversity. Using training modules sent from the Washington office was right up my alley because it connected me to people. The modules showed how to get started with a diversity presentation, provided icebreakers, and established the agency's definition of diversity, which included creating a culturally diverse workforce in which employees of differing race, sex, and national origin had opportunities to advance and contribute. A more comprehensive definition would develop in the next few years to include religion, marital status, color, people with disabilities, and, ultimately, sexual orientation.[11]

We were well on our way to widening that spectrum of inclusion, and my job included educating the rural macho Forest Service workforce in Montana about talking with people different from them. The modules included excerpts from interviews, video examples, reading lists, and lists of videos primarily about men and women working together. One module introduced the idea of differing cultural communication styles, such as a ranger speaking with a Native American. We Americans teach our youth to communicate by looking people in the eye because it indicates confidence. Native people and Asians are taught that quiet respect is most powerful; it is disrespectful to look directly at someone. Learning about those differences teaches us culturally respectful ways to interact. I also presented information that explained stereotypes, ways to identify personal biases, and about body language messages.

This is where I came face-to-face with the true character of the Forest Service I had joined. Many white men did not take my presentations very well, and not only because of the color of my skin. No one ever said anything to me personally; my knowledge came from district female employees, who told me the men disliked hearing about diversity or taking women or non-foresters into the field. Diversity training exacerbated their resentment of women and "ologists." These field guys were used to coming into the office, getting a briefing on their projects and a daily safety training, and heading out independently. Foresters don't go out in the field without discussing what the hazards might be for that day. If it's summertime, there could be bees; in the winter, roads could be dangerous. If someone had seen a bear, that would come out in the briefing. The umbrella name for this was Safety First. These were men who preferred being in the woods to spending time around a lot of people, men who believed in "getting out the cut." They were rough, tough guys who believed women belonged in offices, not on fire lines, and people of color belonged in cities, not on their work crews. But they had no choice—the WO mandated the training. My job was to expand their ideas, and help them understand two things: (1) the Forest Service required them to change their ways of thinking, and (2) their leadership believed diversity would strengthen the Forest Service.

Many men hunted, fished, shot guns for fun, and chewed tobacco. I did none of these things. I was an African American and a city girl. I would stand there with my hands on my hips and start by joking: "Now guys. Imagine what it would be like to go to the woods with me, someone who is very different from you—without this training." They would look at me surprised, like *we'd never do that*, but they knew what I meant. "Let's say I show up on the district and I want to go out in the woods with you: What would you think? How would you react? This training will help you to respond." I tried to endear myself to them. "This is not pulling teeth, guys," I'd say. And it usually worked. I was gutsy and I was charming. By making them laugh, I connected with some of these macho men. I was a good presenter who taught them the value of diversity, partly just by being myself.

As a tactic, I asked districts to have a potluck before the trainings, because I know food loosens people up. This way I could carry some humanity into a situation that likely felt uncomfortable for them. Everyone had accepted their assigned roles until then. Women belonged in the office, men in the field. Many of them had never even talked with a black person. They knew nothing of the world outside of their own small-town, white, rural bubble. Most simply lacked exposure to people of color, like the little girl who told her mommy that I needed to wash my face. Others harbored hatred. I knew the difference. Ignorance and malice showed in the body language and condescending tones of some of the people I met, those who'd look away, whose angry faces revealed white supremacist attitudes. I'd spent a lot of time around white people in the WO, and I could feel the negative vibrations from those who didn't want to interact with me.

I tried to remember that people are basically good and that if I showed them respect, I would get the same in return. I had to learn to communicate with these guys, and it wasn't easy. I could not stereotype them as hicks or backward because of where they came from. They were professional foresters and technicians. Nor did I want them to stereotype me. I had to model a shared humanity and stand in front of them without judgment. Getting to know them before I spoke created relationships that left me unafraid. Still, I knew there were some obstinates who would never accept me, or anyone different. That sometimes made me feel like a fox surrounded by hounds. I recall at one of the potlucks, just before a

diversity training, I overheard someone saying, "She'd make good shooting practice." But I knew that guy didn't represent the majority, and I felt
like person-to-person contact could change some people's minds and
hearts. As I learned about who they were, that their world had not previously been influenced by outsiders, I developed some empathy. Because I
made those human connections, word got out not to kill the messenger.
Besides, the Forest Service resembled the military in some ways. The rank
and file knew they had to support whatever came down from the WO.

In addition to mandatory diversity trainings, the agency started holding larger conferences to educate the workforce. One of these conferences
took place in Coeur d'Alene, Idaho, home to the Aryan Nation, then and
now. I gave a speech there about how I felt as a minority in the agency,
and how important it is to believe in and love yourself. Conference orga-
nizers also brought in major speakers like Derrick Bell, the famous African American Harvard professor who drew attention to the university's
lack of diversity through a 1987 office sit-in, the same year he published
And We Are Not Saved: The Elusive Quest for Racial Justice. Bell spoke at
other conferences in the Northwest, as did Byron Kunisawa, a Japanese
American man born in an internment camp, who grew up with black
people in Oakland, California. These types of speakers not only educated
employees about race, they also inspired many of us to stand firm about
racial justice and become our best selves.

Despite the good feelings at the conference, Forest Service leaders
knew they were holding this event in the heart of a state riddled with
white nationalists, so the agency's law enforcement was out in full force.
They told me not to leave the hotel—for my own safety. I thought that
was absurd. I knew there was a black female lawyer who lived in Coeur
d'Alene who came back and forth to the conference daily. The Forest Service didn't know how to handle hatred. I'd had experience with it. That
little girl came back—you say no, I say yes. No one was going to tell me to
stay put, so I snuck out one evening to prove to myself that Forest Service
anxiety about race was overdone. It was around six at night, and all I did
was walk around the hotel's neighborhood. No one smiled at me. They
just stared, with some nodding now and then. In retrospect, I realize it
was a stupid thing to do, and I was lucky nothing happened.

Home Life and Community in Montana

Not everything in Montana was work- or race-related. My children and I met some friends we really liked in Missoula. Arlen Roll and his wife, Meryl, stand out, as does Sherry Munther, ranger on the Nine Mile District, and her husband, Greg. These people provided me with a social life outside the Forest Service and a safety net I didn't know I needed. Arlen, who found our house for us before we arrived, worked in personnel and had greeted me the day I arrived. He clearly tried to ensure our comfort. Sherry was one of the best facilitators I had ever met. When she and I held public meetings together, we really connected. I recall going to her house, where she made me yummy seven-grain cereal like I'd never had before. We all became friends. A few times we ate together, often we laughed together.

In DC, I'd had a mostly white life in the office and a black life at home, in my church, with my family, and in my neighborhood. It was good to find close friendships with white people in Missoula, where I could just be me, to feel like more than just a black person in a totally white place. The times with Arlen and Meryl Roll were like that. I had friends that took me bowling, and we did other things I'd never done before, like drinking microbrews and hiking on forest trails. I had drunk hard alcohol sparingly before, but never beer. People in Montana loved their microbrews, they loved their sports, and they loved their fishing and hunting. It was a different world, and I was excited to be part of it. I even hiked up the trail to the "M" on the side of the hill near the University of Montana.

Missoula was a time for multiple awakenings. I volunteered in the community by joining the Soroptimists, the business and professional women's association. I was even appointed to an acting vacant seat on the board of the Blue Mountain Women's Clinic. I'd never been on a board before and loved it! Activities outside the Forest Service helped me to better understand where I lived, including the Mormon influence in town. I also volunteered at a battered women's shelter, work that spoke to my heart. The shelter took me away from my Forest Service persona and the pressures of daily assessment at work. There, I could talk woman-to-woman and simply present myself as Gloria. It connected me to women whose lives were far worse than my own, and taught me about the many ways people interpret love. Sometimes husbands learned where their wives and children were and some went home to their abusive husbands even before their bruises healed. I often felt a combination of sadness, anger, empathy, and understanding. The community work added meaning to my life beyond home and Forest Service.

The job was going great and I was settling in, despite the fact I could not find products for my hair and sometimes a grocery store clerk treated me differently than the white person in front of me. I didn't like it, but I believed this was probably as bad as Missoula would get. All this I could handle. It was different when bigotry affected my children. I became Mother Bear, ready to attack. For most of our Montana year, we all did very well, although everything seemed the opposite of DC in Montana, from the clothes people wore—flats versus heels—to the conversations they had—cows and guns versus cars and dancing. My son couldn't find shoes big enough for his size-13 feet, so we ordered them from a catalogue. He was 6 feet, 5 inches tall and played sports, so he blended nicely into Montana's culture. He also learned how to shoot a rifle with my friend, Arlen. I felt concerned, especially when Arlen told me, "He's a natural." Having lived on the East Coast, determined to keep my boy away from trouble, I didn't want to hear that. Every time he went out, I gave him a stern lecture about why I would never allow guns in our home. He loved shooting, but after Montana I never heard another word about it.

My sixteen-year-old middle girl, Catrina, was like sunshine coming out of a storm, a true optimist, always a smile on her face and very protective of her sister and brother. She had one true friend in Missoula, an American Indian girl. To this day, Catrina feels certain that if our worst-case scenario hadn't happened, they'd have made more friends, that coming into a brand-new high school is tough for any teenager. In retrospect, I think I did the kids a disservice by not giving them more consideration before moving to Missoula. We talked about having them stay with my parents, but I wouldn't have gone without them, and they knew it. They didn't want to move to Missoula. What they didn't know is that I did it for them. Later in life they told me their Missoula experience helped shape who they became.

Our Worst-Case Scenario

I had wanted to advance, and I had wanted out of the city. We lived in an apartment with mice in DC. Now we had a rodent-free three-bedroom house. Boys hung out on the stoops in DC. Now we had a backyard and fresh air. In DC, my girls had to ignore whistles from grown men as they came home. This was the street culture, where people lazed around and sat on stoops drinking, smoking, doing nothing constructive in the middle of the day and through the night. People drove cars in Missoula. They walked everywhere or took the bus in DC. In Montana, the kids smoked cigarettes, chewed tobacco, and drove up and down the streets for the fun of it, "cruising." My kids did not like the beer drinking and country music, but life felt more stable, less dangerous in Missoula. That's what I wanted for them, a nice life. Yes, moving was hard, but it might have been harder to keep them out of trouble in the city. We could adjust to the cultural changes, but I hadn't considered that my kids had never lived as minorities. Missoula changed that. In Missoula, my children learned that white people liked to claim they had black friends, but did not really want to know them. They also learned that racism was always lying just beneath the surface, ready to explode unexpectedly.

One of those eruptions changed our lives the day the female basketball captain forcibly threw my oldest daughter, Nicki, against the lockers, repeatedly punched her in the back, and called her a nigger. Nicki was a senior, beautiful and quick to join the in-crowd, the pretty girls whose parents had money. She was not a fighter. But, when she heard that word, she came undone, broke loose from the teacher, and attacked. Both girls were suspended, but the school blamed Nicki for the fight, a squabble that had started the previous day. That N-word was telling. We'd all heard it before, but never as often as in Missoula, where it always came from the young people. That day, the word and the sentiment behind it burst into light. The basketball captain's face bled from being scratched. Nicki's bruises were severe, but no one saw them because of her clothes.

When Catrina came home from school a few days later and reported that the basketball captain was practicing at school for a game in Kalispell, Mother Bear came out. That girl had attacked my daughter, who was at home because of the suspension. As always, I did my research. The school's rule book said that suspended students could not participate in extracurricular activities, so I called for a meeting with the principal. When I got to the school, the vice principal met with me. After some small talk, I asked why the school was allowing the basketball captain to practice and play in the upcoming game, while Nicki remained suspended. He responded nicely, complimenting me on my role in the community, and then he said, "Mrs. Brown, we didn't have this kind of problem before your children arrived."

I knew exactly what that meant. All of the stereotypes about African Americans and violence came crashing down around me. I was in shock. I got up, walked out, and did not look back. This was my biggest fear come true. We lived in a place where people were nice to us but called us the N-word behind our backs. Now the kids were hearing that word every day in the school hallway. It was my worst-case scenario. People who had power over my children interpreted their every move in light of negative, media-induced views of black culture. Most had never met an African American before. What was I to do? First, I thought about my dead husband, to whom I had always looked for protection. What would he suggest? Then, I called my mother. "Bring my grandbabies home," she said. Well, that wasn't going to happen. I would not be separated from my children, and I had a good job with a future. After I hung up, I sobbed with the pillow over my head so that Andre, Catrina, and Nicki wouldn't hear me.

When I returned to work the next day, my coworkers noticed that I wasn't the bright, chatty Gloria they knew. They asked what was wrong, but I didn't want to cry, so I lied. I told them I was coming down with something. All I could think is, *I'm in a fire no one can put out.* That day at lunch I told one of my closest friends what had happened. He was mortified. "Gloria," he said, "This is not Missoula." But he was wrong. It *was* Missoula, just not the town he experienced as a white man. Later, I got a call from Jim Overbay, the regional forester, to come to his office. I thought he wanted to talk about the civil rights video I was working on, so I made sure I was prepared. To my surprise, he asked me what happened at the school.

After I returned to my desk, I received a call from the principal of Sentinel High School, who asked for a meeting. Jim Overbay had reached out to the superintendent of public schools. I agreed, so long as he did not include his vice principal. I met him after work and told the story again. The principal apologized profusely, and then explained that the school had gone easy on the student because of concern for her safety. She had an abusive father, and her brothers often came to school with bruises and black eyes. The student's extended family lived in Kalispell and looked forward to seeing her play. The administration feared that if her father knew she started the fight, he might hurt her. Holding back tears, I responded. "I am a mother, too. If you had included me, maybe I'd have understood. But," I asked, "Did anyone think about how this would affect my daughter? Do you see how this looks like discrimination to me?"

He told me the truth. "No."

I'd heard enough. The principal did not recognize that he treated my daughter differently *because* she was black. I knew how to recognize these kinds of latent discriminatory acts (called microaggressions by Derrick Bell) because I had seen and experienced them before. I thanked him for his time, got up, and left without looking back. Nicki headed to DC to spend her senior year with my mother, in a more comfortable environment.

Leaving Montana

Missoula no longer felt like a great place to be. I had enjoyed so much of my life there, but when Catrina told me how unhappy she and Andre were also, I knew we had to go. The agency facilitated a transfer to Region 6 in Portland, Oregon. Thankfully, the Forest Service pays for station transfers when an employee takes a job at least a hundred miles away. This was true for all eight moves I made, except when I retired. This time I had movers. They were big, husky fellows, with freckles and seemed typical of Montana—they grow them big! They were friendly and professional, although they did joke with Nicki, who had returned to drive with me to Portland. The other two children had gone to visit their grandparents in Silver Spring, Maryland, while Nicki and I reconnected.

I knew we would go into temporary quarters while we looked for a permanent residence, so we packed everything we thought we would need until we found our new home. I also included all the wonderful gifts I'd received at my going-away party. I knew that some people had only come for the food, but others came to give me a sincere send-off, with stories and words of affection. My most enduring present came from a very true friend. It was a reproduction of a Charles Russell painting that still hangs in my home. One of my last acts was to catch up on the mail I had ignored for days.

The newspaper had printed an in-depth article in the July 21, 1987, issue of the *Missoulian* about why I was leaving, and I was receiving mail from strangers. The article, titled "Shades of Racism," pointed to both the hospitality and the discrimination we had faced there from the first day. A lot of people told me in their letters, "This is not Montana." Unfortunately, the Montana they knew and the place we experienced differed significantly. One letter stood out. Richard Ford, a writer from Mississippi, was white, but his words confirmed and soothed my inner anguish. Being an outsider was not a problem for him, but he understood Montana's insularity and expressed my deepest pain by writing, "I know that in the life of raising children and being a single parent, such a mood—exacerbated by racism—would soon grow intolerable. . . . I regret your experience and am sorry for the unhappiness it's caused you." His articulation of our experience warmed my heart.[12]

I felt sad about leaving. I had been naïve about Montana, but I'd also learned that if I set my mind to it, I could do just about anything. I had ridden a horse, set up camp, cooked outdoors, learned to fight fire, made new friends in an all-white community, helped other women, and begun to focus on civil rights. When I arrived, the beauty of Big Sky Country had enveloped me like a blanket. Now I felt cold.

CHAPTER 3

In the Land of Spotted Owls and Salmon

I WOKE UP TO A BEAUTIFUL BOLD SUNNY DAY. The sky looked painted into an artsy form of heaven, mesmerizingly filled with shades of blue. Despite its beauty, today I would leave Missoula, Montana, the Big Sky Country, with little regret. It would be easy to leave the past behind, because the worst-case scenario—severe racism—had reached into our home. Nothing could top seeing my children traumatized because of the color of their skin.

From a career standpoint, Missoula had been good; I had needed the training and I appreciated the opportunities I found in the West. I had learned about fire suppression, wilderness and recreation, public speaking, speechwriting, video production, and much more. I finally felt integrated into the agency, worthy of being a professional.

I wanted more.

In Montana, the mountains had become my home, no longer far-off entities to drive through or visit. I had so many firsts in Missoula—I knew we had to go, but I felt melancholy about leaving my friends behind, both inside and outside the Forest Service. Some friends had admitted after a few microbrews that they'd never had a black friend before. I told them that it was weird for me to have only white friends. I had never lived in an all-white society, just worked in it during the day. I remember thinking, *I will never again live in an all-white society.* I was headed to Portland, where at least there was *some* black community. Only at the end of my career would I finally acknowledge that I'd become part of the white realm, that I would likely spend the rest of my life in a white world.

It was never easy to be the only African American in the room, but it was common in the Forest Service West. My optimistic nature often carried me through the isolation and underlying discrimination in those days. I was—and am—a people person with good intuition. I relied on my smile and friendliness, regardless of how people responded. Doing the best job I could was always a priority. Only later did I realize that what it took to survive was courage, a willingness to listen and understand, sensitivity, and a thick skin.

Reunions and Connections

We had an uneventful drive from Missoula to Portland, one that gave me time alone with my daughter, time that we needed. I had not seen Nicki for months. I had missed a lot, moments I can never recover. I couldn't help but think that racism meant I had missed my daughter's once-in-a-lifetime prom, Christmas, and her graduation. In those days before Skype and FaceTime, it took weeks to even get a picture developed. I had missed seeing her face on a daily basis, and skipping those important life events really broke my heart. But I couldn't afford to take all of us to DC for even one of those events, and I could not leave my other children alone in Montana.

The road trip gave us time to talk, space to heal. Nicki told me about her year, about Christmas, her prom date, and the family at graduation. I told her that my job was taking us into unknown territory again. None of us knew what to expect, but we needed to give it a chance. I told her that I knew moving was hard, but we had been through a lot already, tragedy and the challenges of moving into a white community. We could do it. This had to be easier, because at least there were other African Americans in Portland. I also told her honestly that Oregon is very white, and we still needed thick skin. You can't interpret every action or behavior as prejudicial, but you do have to stand up for yourself. You must always confront racism head-on.

I don't remember much about the scenery during that drive. The Columbia River Gorge is one of the most striking landscapes in the country, with sheer cliffs rising high above the massive river that slowly wends its way toward the sea. I didn't even notice the stark transition from tumbleweeds, basalt cliffs, and rolling synclines to glimpses of the few evergreen trees that almost magically transition to a densely forested landscape past The Dalles. I saw that only later, when we visited Multnomah Falls, got ice cream in Hood River, and drove a little farther east. I'm sure I would have remembered that landscape if Nicki and I had not been so emotionally entwined.

I do remember arriving in Portland. The skies were sunny, and it wasn't raining like everyone had warned! We went straight to our temporary housing, an apartment building on the Willamette River waterfront. The movers put my furniture in storage, and for the next few weeks Nicki and I explored the neighborhood, identifying our favorite shops and restaurants in preparation for Andre and Catrina. When Nicki and I finally headed to the airport to pick them up, I felt giddy, like Christmas and my birthday together. That night, we went to dinner at a restaurant within walking distance from our apartment and celebrated my pretend birthday. I recall feeling thrilled: dinner in Portland for my birthday, a place with an African American population; my dreams and goals of getting to R-6 coming true; all my children back together. Life couldn't get much better!

The next day I enrolled my children in school. I took Catrina and Andre to Lincoln High, and Nicki and I met with Margaret Carter. At the time, Margaret worked as a counselor for Portland Community College, Cascade Campus. I remember clearly our breakfast at the Village Inn Restaurant on Broadway in Northeast Portland. The restaurant had been at the same location since 1958 and is still there, though it's pretty dingy now, in my opinion. Margaret asked Nicki a lot of questions to help determine the best placement for her. Then she helped us with Nicki's application and in choosing and scheduling classes. Margaret guided us through this process and then took care of everything. She said Nicki should be prepared to start her first class in September, unless she heard otherwise.

Margaret and I hit it off like old friends from the moment we met and remained close throughout her political career. It had been such a relief to have an African American woman ease our entry to Portland. We had a lot in common. Margaret was born in Shreveport, Louisiana, in

1935 and escaped an abusive husband to come to Portland at thirty-two years old, with her five children. She had returned to college for a bachelor's degree in education and a master's in educational psychology. She didn't stop there. In 1984, she became the first African American woman elected to the Oregon State Legislature. She continued in the State House for twenty-eight years and moved to the State Senate in 2000.[1] Margaret Carter was a very smart individual, who had never met a stranger, and she was a survivor like me. I admired her.

I couldn't imagine a better start for us all. Margaret was important in the African American community and a gracious, kind person, informal but very elegant at the same time. She had no trouble interacting with her congressional peers at formal affairs outside the legislature. She also put forth legislative bills that mattered to her constituents. There I was, coming in from outside, and she made my welcome feel special. I had not grown up in the neighborhood like most of her friends, but they let me in as well, and I found it comforting. For the first time since leaving DC, we were among other African Americans who were doing very, very well, part of a strong community. It made me realize just how hard it had been in Montana, where I had to represent *all* African Americans. I had to look good all the time. Portland was so much easier. I was no longer alone.

I also learned about Oregon's own ugly history. Many of the early settlers came from the South, and they carried their prejudices with them. In fact, Oregon passed a law before statehood that allowed people to bring slaves in and keep them in the territory for up to three years. Then the slaves had to leave or they could be whipped. The "lash law" did not last long, but the Oregon State Constitution banned "Negroes," free or slave, in 1859. That was long ago, and things had changed by the time I arrived, but more recently I learned that the state didn't ratify the equal-protection Fourteenth Amendment of the US Constitution until 1973![2]

African Americans had been discouraged from coming to Oregon, and there weren't many of us here, but World War II increased the state's black population by bringing people to work in the shipyards. This meant that the people I met had grown up in a place that, first, did not allow Blacks into the state, and then made all kinds of rules to make them uncomfortable once they were there. For example, African Americans in Oregon had higher car insurance rates than Whites and experienced overtly racist places like the Coon Chicken Inn. Then there were the

"Whites-only" restaurants and the redlining of housing, which continued legally into the 1950s and informally up to the 1990s. Most African
Americans I met lived in Northeast Portland because that's the part of the
city that allowed them after the war.

I had these conversations and learned about this past, but these
things didn't affect my day-to-day life much. At least we could move
around without skin color at the front of our minds every single moment.
Portland was on the West Coast, but included a close-knit, black, middle-
class community and six or seven different churches that provided activities. There were dances, get-togethers, and theater. What really struck me
is that white people mixed into that world. I had never seen white people
at a black church before. Despite the racist undertones, it was far better
for my family than Missoula, Montana.

Portland presented other types of openness I had never seen: I saw
both interracial couples and overt homosexuality for the first time. Being
gay was still generally hidden then. The 1980s had birthed a lot of openness, mainly in California, that you wouldn't have found on the east side
of Oregon. But there it was in Portland: visually obvious homosexuality.
Same-sex couples held hands and even kissed in public. I recall one time
I went to a bar and found that everyone there was gay.

One thing I didn't know then, but do now, is that Forest Service led
the way in the Department of Agriculture on policies related to sexual
orientation. A report on harassment and discrimination faced by gay and
lesbian employees in California and the Northwest had pointed out that
sexual orientation was "conspicuously absent" in civil rights publications
and harassment policies. Chief Dale Robertson responded by seeking
training for equal employment opportunity counselors from the Department of Agriculture. He even told them the Forest Service would "continue moving forward" by incorporating sexual orientation into training
and diversity issues. I remember the openness of the community, but I
had no idea that the chief of the Forest Service had included sexual orientation in the agency's no-harassment policy and, by 1993, successfully
urged the Department of Agriculture to do the same.[3]

This was a time when all kinds of diversity issues bubbled to the
surface, mirroring shifts in a lot of employment sectors. Still, the Forest
Service employed very few people of color—only 13 percent of the entire
workforce in 1988; 4 percent were African American, the same proportion

as today.[4] More civil rights conferences were held in Oregon, like the one I had attended in Idaho, but I don't remember much about them because I was so busy learning about my new job and raising my teenagers.

When the kids arrived, it was time to find a permanent home. We looked primarily in Northeast Portland, the African American part of town. We saw one house on NE Siskiyou that we loved, with a great big yard, front and back, and shrubs that shielded it from the view of neighbors. I knew it was too expensive, but I went to look anyway. My house in Montana and those in Oregon were all made of wood, but my homes back east had all been made of brick, so there were some architectural differences. One of the things I had really liked in DC, part of the regional culture, was sitting on the porch and watching people pass by. There was a porch at the Siskiyou house.

Then, we visited a house on Portland Boulevard (later Rosa Parks Way). It was affordable and just right for my large family. This one belonged to the Stoudamires, a well-known Portland African American family, whose son Damon played professional basketball. The house was gray and yellow and stood out from the others on the block. It was huge, with four bedrooms, three bathrooms, and a large kitchen, dining room, and living room. It had been built in the 1950s and had a new roof, new appliances, and a small yard. This meant low maintenance, something I liked as a single parent. The clincher was that this front porch extended from one side of the house to the other, a great place to sit and watch people pass. I made an offer, and we moved in right away. Now that everyone was settled, it was time to get back to work.

The Portland Regional Office

I will always remember my first day on the job. I had a new boss, Jerry Gause, director of information for the Pacific Northwest. I had met Jerry when I worked for RPA and he came to the WO for a detail. Jerry was tall, with perfect dark hair, and very handsome, always in a nice suit. He stood out to me in DC because he dressed well, and his crisp white shirts always looked brand-new. Jerry reminded me of a military man, the kind who knew how to greet you with a charming smile and a firm handshake that told you not to mess with him, stoic and at all times professional.

Most Forest Service guys are not the hugging kind, and Jerry was no exception. But I was so happy to see him, and so excited all around, that I hugged him. Boy, was that a mistake! In those days, I was always colorfully dressed to the nines, in heels and a dress or skirt and blouse, my hair and makeup impeccably done. Not only is dressing up part of my cultural norms as an African American woman, but I also knew that, in this white world, people would notice me because of the color of my skin. So, I never tried to hide myself away. If they were going to look at me, I was going to look good! That meant wearing my best color on my lips—bright red. That red lipstick and Jerry's white shirt are forever etched in my mind, because when I hugged him the lipstick stayed on his collar. *All day long.* I spent the rest of the day hoping and praying that he wouldn't see himself in the mirror. I was mortified, so embarrassed that if I had been white, I would have stayed red until the weekend. Always the gentleman, Jerry never said a word.

I also connected with my immediate supervisor, Sherry Wagner, whom I'd met when I went to St. Anthony, Idaho, on my *pretending-I-did-not-have-butterflies-in-my-stomach* detail. We also knew one another from her detail at the WO, where we worked on a project reviewing and documenting public response to the latest national Resource Planning Act (RPA) assessment documents. Sherry was a trained mathematician, but Forest Service did not hire mathematicians, so she moved through the agency as one of our smartest information specialists. I lost track of her after she became director of information in Region 9, Milwaukee, Wisconsin, but I later learned she became the civil rights director in the Pacific Northwest.

The Portland RO had a lot more employees than the regional office in Missoula, probably because R-6 timber harvests provided additional operating money. These revenues increased opportunities for advancement beyond anywhere else in the National Forest System, my main reason for being there. There was a lot more to do in R-6 than in R-1. I had higher levels of responsibility, did deeper research and writing, and interacted more with the public than ever before.

I knew I had come to the right place because the job suited my ambitions perfectly. The work of a public affairs specialist at a GS-11 professional pay scale included writing memos, preparing internal PowerPoint presentations for the leadership team, reviewing and editing environmental and other documents, giving speeches, and preparing briefing books for show-me trips. A lot of environmental laws had been passed from the mid-1970s through the late 1980s. Many of them manifested in R-6 and, ultimately, led to the turbulent times that shaped my career. Like my experience at the WO, these years in public affairs provided me the background to become an agency leader. During those early days in Portland, I knew I was ready to move up!

I was eager to talk with John Butruille, the regional forester and my last boss before leaving the WO, about a strategy for achieving my next position. But John reminded me that I needed to focus on learning my current job well, not just what comes next. *Good!* I thought. *I'll excel at this job* and *I'll strategize for my future at the same time.* I was still in money-making mode to support my family and had to keep my goals front and center, at least in my own mind. Taking care of the family financially was my main priority and always had been since I lost Willie James. I did not start really appreciating the work that Forest Service did, and my role in the bigger picture of the agency's mission, until later in my career.

Environmental Issues in Region 6

I spent the first two weeks in Portland studying up on issues like the spotted owl, salmon, timber, wilderness, recreation, and public involvement—just the tip of the iceberg when it came to learning about R-6. I also became much more aware of what it means to "get out the cut." Region 6 had harvested 5.8 billion board feet (bbf) of timber in 1988 and regularly produced a third or more of the nation's timber, even though it is one of nine regions in the country.[5] This massive timber production catalyzed the major issues I faced—conflicts with environmentalists who tried to stop everything from timber sales to production of the region's national forest plans. The 1976 National Forest Management Act (NFMA) had pushed the agency to recognize more value in land use than just timber harvests, which meant forest plans had to include all types of users, from people cutting cordwood or harvesting special forest products like moss to people riding horses, motorbikes, or snowmobiles. Together with the National Environmental Policy Act of 1969, the NFMA mandated public involvement in decision-making processes. This is where I would find my niche—working with environmental groups and the public.

One of my first assignments was to prepare a briefing paper on public feedback from the draft regional forest plan, the document that set the direction for managing land and resources on all the national forests in Oregon and Washington. The draft environmental impact statement (EIS) for the proposed forest plans had been released in 1987, and John Butruille became regional forester two years later, a time when issues related to timber supply, old-growth forests, spotted owls, and salmon were prominent. Feedback on the plans came from industry, environmental groups, and the public at large, and responses varied widely. Industry wanted to continue or increase harvests. Environmental groups wanted to halt timber production altogether, especially that related to clear-cutting, and they had ecosystem science to back them up. Between 1990 and 1995, regional timber harvests were reduced first to 3.8 bbf and then to fewer than a billion board feet. And the public wanted multiple use of managed lands: horseback riding, bicycle and motorcycle trails, camping, fishing, and hiking. The problem was often overlapping stakeholder desires at the same sites.

When the time came to present the public feedback to the regional leadership team (RLT), Sherry let me do it. The team included the regional forester, his two deputies, and all the forest supervisors and their deputies. I wasn't afraid until I saw their body language. As I spoke, I watched some of them lean back, arms crossed. Others looked around the room or down at the ground, not at me. In those days, the Forest Service did not like environmentalists, and was very close with the timber industry. These foresters disliked hearing about the impact of their practices on old-growth ecosystems. Not only that, these high-level foresters and engineers considered themselves the experts. They knew how to manage forests just fine, thank you very much, and had been doing it for more than three-quarters of a century. Efficiency had been the agency's middle name, and the RLT was proud of that reputation. They did not appreciate public input if it meant reducing productivity.

The region's timber mission had collided with public expectations, especially as definitions of what constituted agency stakeholders expanded. I was not vested in these decades-old attitudes that made them defensive, so I didn't sugarcoat the message about necessary changes and crafted public responses that were not industry-only. I realized once again that most of these guys were not open to any message that changed the status quo. I had seen the same response when talking about diversity in Montana. These men clearly loathed anything that "threatened" how they managed the timber program, including scientific evidence or any suggestion of diminishing old-growth harvests. I remember thinking, *Please don't shoot the messenger.* My supervisor gave me positive feedback that I had done a good job on my presentation, but I didn't know whether I had really gotten through to the leadership team. Afterward, I kept wishing I were a fly on the wall to witness the heated conversations that I am sure ensued.

For my next big task, I coordinated with the Siuslaw National Forest on an upcoming show-me trip for folks from the Washington office. In 1989, the chief had released a New Perspectives initiative based on ecosystem management, and the Washington office employees were coming to witness implementation on the ground and report back to the chief. They wanted to see a project related to the spotted owl and/or salmon. The owl favored old-growth forests, and the fish needed habitat that included downed logs and pools. Forest Service previously believed we needed to clean debris out of rivers, but scientists had begun to understand the importance of leaving organic matter in rivers and streams. Downed logs and other woody debris protected fish by creating nutrient-filled pools that also provided cover, habitat, and cooling, especially important for juvenile fish.[6] As scientists learned more, and with laws to protect air and water that also required public input, we started putting logs back into rivers. We also had to follow new rules to accommodate the owl populations when we did timber sales.

Show-me trips take a lot of organizing. I had to coordinate with visiting WO directors—timber, wildlife and fish, their counterparts in the regional office, and the forest supervisor. Most importantly, I had to connect with the district staff to make arrangements and determine the best sites to visit. Finally, we had to agree internally about the take-home message for higher-ups. The forest supervisor, rangers, and staff selected the projects we would see. We were on the precipice of ecosystem management and focused on increasing biodiversity, drawing battle lines over timber versus recreation versus environment. It was my job to work on messaging. The forest staff described project design, and I tied everyday language into the regional and Washington office briefing books. I had to make sure the message matched party-line expectations without offending the timber industry.

Silver Lake Detail

Later that month, Arlen Roll called me from Montana to ask if I would be interested in a ranger detail to a district office. The detail did not provide me a promotion to ranger, but the assignment would give me experience as a practicing ranger. Arlen had made a request from one of his friends, Ollie Sheldon, forest supervisor of the Fremont-Winema National Forest in Oregon. I was eager and a little scared when Ollie called to offer me the acting district ranger position at the Silver Lake Ranger District on the Fremont National Forest. I had never traveled to Eastern Oregon, and I had heard it was very conservative and much whiter than Portland. But any friend of mine knows I'd want to share my skills, and that fear would never stop me from taking on a challenge.

Silver Lake was an unincorporated city, located seventy-five miles southeast of Bend and ninety-five miles north of the headquarters office in Lakeview, Oregon. I remember my drive there clearly. I headed south on I-5 in my Forest Service vehicle and then, outside Eugene, took OR-58 past Oakridge. The remainder of the trip took me through more forests than towns. After 262 miles and four and a half lonely hours, I reached my destination just after dusk. I decided to drive through town, rather than heading straight to the district. The town had no stoplights, and the tour took about ten minutes from one end to the other. When I reached the eastern edge of town, I turned around and headed for the district. A few minutes later I saw someone standing in the middle of the road waving his hands. It was a police officer! I had not seen him parked on the side of the road in the dark. I stopped and put down my window. "What can I do for you, officer?" I asked.

He said, "You lost?"

"No," I said.

"I saw you drive through town and turn around. Sure you're not lost?"

"I'm the new district ranger," I told him. "I just arrived from Portland."

As I let this sink in, his eyes became wider. His mouth dropped open and we just stared. It was long enough to be funny, but I knew better than to laugh.

Finally, he said, "Ah, umm, well, yes, we play baseball with Forest Service employees."

I said, "That's nice, officer, I look forward to seeing you at the games."

After another long pause he said, "I guess you have to get along now?"

"Yes, thank you, officer," I replied. "I do need to go meet my staff and employees."

He turned, left the middle of the road, and got into his car in the shadows. *Hmmm,* I thought. *He did not tell me his name and he didn't ask for mine. How strange.* As I drove to the district, it sank in. *This encounter wasn't odd at all. As a black woman in the white West, I should be used to responses like this by now.* But I resolved never to become used to those kinds of reactions. I would always lead with a smile and hope that people would recognize me for who I am, rather than the color of my skin.

I had an opportunity to put that expectation into practice almost immediately. As I pulled into the district, I saw employees peering out the window. I guess everyone wanted to see me arrive, the first black woman in charge of their district—a place that had always been run by white men. I put on my most positive persona and pulled up my strongest mind-set. I smiled, asked questions, remembered their names and used them, and performed as though I was glad to be there, regardless of my feelings. I expected the same in return.

Silver Lake Ranger District was a true old-time Forest Service compound. The district office and a fleet of cars were within the complex, where all the employees lived and worked. About thirty single-family houses were occupied by married employees and families. Summertime temp workers and single folks stayed in the two bunkhouses. The district ranger got the main house. That was me now.

The next morning, I dressed in my Forest Service pickle suit, plus badge and boots. Everything was green, even my socks. I didn't see any green underwear in the catalogue but was told that's what real foresters wore, so I brought my own. That morning I headed to the main building to meet everyone, including the children. I gave a brief speech about who I was and how I got my assignment. Their greetings seemed sincere. Next thing I knew, Jim Anderson, the timber staff officer, hustled me away to my office.

Although the protocol is unwritten, as usual with new leadership, the entire management team waited to greet me. Each of them later briefed me individually. Meanwhile, the group addressed everything from timber sales to special use permits, and drew my attention to issues that needed immediate attention. For example, Mrs. Western refused to control her dog's barking at night. I found this amusing, and at the same time admired that the team's description of the compound and their duties sounded like a well-oiled machine. I was impressed with their level of detail and knowledge of the land. They had been leaderless for almost two months; yet, their work had continued without a hitch.

It was clear to me that district employees took the agency mission to heart: "To sustain the health, diversity, and productivity of the nation's forests and grasslands to meet the needs of present and future generations." When I first worked for the Forest Service, this statement had been summed up by the motto "The greatest good for the greatest number in the long run," but by the time I got to the Northwest, it had become "Caring for the Land, Serving People." These employees reflected the Forest Service way—efficiency, pride, independence, and dedication to their work. They continued doing their jobs with or without a ranger. I realized that although we need a hierarchy of leadership at the forest, regional, and WO levels, we could all rely on the fact that district-level employees know what they're supposed to do, and they do it well.

Honoring the mandate of caring for the land and serving people is how the twenty employees at Silver Lake conducted themselves. Including their families, forty-nine people lived on the Forest Service compound in this community of fewer than two hundred. With summertime temp workers, the district housed as many as sixty-five people. This meant close connections between the Forest Service and the community. The people on this district were very proud of their volcano education and recreational programs, which centered on camping, fishing, hunting, bird-watching, and woodcutting. These were the very things also appreciated by the people in town. I looked forward to spending the next two months at Silver Lake.

The management team took me on a tour and inspection of the compound and the fleet. This was an opportunity to find out as much as I could about these men and women. Were they married? Did they have children? How long had they lived and worked on the district? What were their professional goals? Did any of them plan to move on? They seemed to appreciate my interest in their families, their goals, and their work. I explained that I was there to listen, learn, and carry out my duties as their "acting" ranger, not dictate to them or make major changes prior to the permanent ranger's arrival.

I also told them, "My words should not suggest weakness, only respect for you and the work you do, and I expect the same from you for me." I spoke softly, but authoritatively, and with friendly words that meant let's get to know each other and have some fun. I was ready to learn from those with experience, and these were the verbatim words suggested by Forest Supervisor Ollie.

The main work on this one-million-acre district dotted with juniper and pine focused on the timber program and removing danger trees—those that blocked road views, were dry, or looked like they might fall down—to reduce biomass for fire management. But now it was time to see what was happening in the field, starting with a new bathroom at Christmas Valley Campground. My all-male leadership presented a review of the environmental assessment (EA) used to document the project. An EA planning document is used when a project presents no known issues or conflicts. If there were major issues or conflict, an environmental impact statement (EIS), requiring far more study and public input, would be needed.

Christmas Valley held ten trailer campsites and a couple of dozen tent camping sites. The campground had been closed for the winter season, but it was time to open again for summer. The campground and trail work had been completed, and all I had to do was sign off on the project. I had no problem with this, since the contractor had clearly adhered to standard Forest Service specs. The bathroom blended in environmentally and holistically with the rest of the campground. And it smelled good; I couldn't help but wonder how long that would last.

I also got to meet the campground hosts, a couple who had been coming to Christmas Valley for nine years. The Forest Service has campground hosts like them all over the nation, usually called snowbirds, meaning they head for sunshine in the winter and return to the mountains and rivers of the West for the summer. Becoming a campground host requires a formal application and, once approved, the hosts—always retirees—can return annually. It's a good deal for everyone. They have a place to live for half the year and get a small stipend for managing the campground. The Forest Service gets near-free labor and two sets of watchful eyes.

My third week on the district, the forest supervisor paid us a visit. I was not surprised, because Ollie and I had been speaking regularly on the phone, but it shocked the district employees. The forest supervisor typically appeared on projects, but had never visited the district office before. His brief remarks included nice words about me. I had been treated well prior to his visit, but I was a hero when Ollie left.

During his visit, we went into the field to observe the first fire of 1989 on the Fremont National Forest. This was the best wildfire training of all, standing atop a cliff where I could see for miles, while Ollie told me how his teams fought the fire. Blazes had erupted all over the eastside, and this one burned everything in sight on the Silver Lake Ranger District. Ollie said the fire had scorched almost a thousand acres. From where we stood on a distant ridge several miles away, we could see firefighters building a fire line, while overhead helicopters dropped red retardant and water directly on the inferno. Ollie taught me a lot about fire as we watched the raging flames. Most fires burn hundreds of acres before they are eventually put out by rain. Our job, he explained, was to keep the fire from getting larger, and to protect homes and resources.

He said that the Forest Service was like a three-legged stool. The legs represented timber, recreation, and fire, each of which plays a role in funding. "You must understand finances if you want to be a line officer," he said. "This knowledge is just as important as field work to carrying out our mission." Agency funding that supports employment and other operations comes from these three legs. Timber harvests pay our bills, recreation is the lifeblood of our support, and we must fight fire to maintain all of the above. Although timber sales provide us the funds for self-support, these three areas determine how you operate your district. Fire is special, though. Because it is inevitable, fire has its own budget. If we get a lightning strike, it's "everyone to the barn" to fight. "I hope this detail helps you to understand the critical role of making decisions and managing people," he told me. Ollie was right about my need for this experience. The two-month detail on the Silver Lake Ranger District gave me an opportunity to work on skills I didn't consciously know I needed. I was glad I had done it. Later, as I traveled back to Portland, I hoped that the new ranger wouldn't have to deal first thing with Mrs. Western and her dogs.

Planning for Advancement

When I returned to Portland, I learned through word of mouth that the Willamette's information officer would soon retire. I decided that might be just the right job for me. It would include more responsibility and a pay raise, because I would move from a GS-12 to a GS-13. I would also sit on the forest management team. I got serious about applying and prepared by reading the Willamette's draft forest plan and following articles in the Eugene *Register-Guard*. The paper often criticized the agency's management of the Willamette National Forest, but the reporting gave me a strong sense of the critical concerns. After I felt like I understood the issues, I decided to meet with Information Officer Jerry Mason, Forest Supervisor Mike Kerrick, and Mike's deputy, Mike Edrington.

Two weeks later I headed to the forest supervisor's office in Eugene, Oregon, about three hours from Portland, and went to Kerrick's office in the federal building. It was springtime, and the drive down reminded me why I loved Oregon. The Willamette Valley shone with life and color, its fields painted with the reds, blues, yellows, and greens of a variety of crops. I traveled a clean highway in bright sunshine, while listening to Willie Nelson and thinking about DC highways. No matter the DC route, cars, trash, and people crowded the area. I definitely did not miss the crowds, the garbage, or the city air. My glorious Oregon drive went quickly, and before I knew it, I arrived. I went straight to the supervisor's office, where I met with Mike K. and Mike E. I was somewhat scared. Forest supervisors are revered, especially this one: Mike Kerrick had achieved the highest allowable timber sales in the nation. During his tenure, it was rumored that the harvest in the Willamette forest headed toward "a billion board feet or bust" of timber per year. At the time, Mike said they were cutting close to seven hundred million board feet.

Mike Kerrick was part of the old-time Forest Service, and his advancement reflected the typical trajectory for a supervisor. He trained in forestry at University of Minnesota in the early 1950s and spent summers on the Willamette's McKenzie River Ranger District. Within two years of his 1954 graduation, he became an assistant district ranger, first on the Blue River Ranger District and then on the Mount Baker National Forest. It took about ten years for him to become a TMA (timber management assistant) at a GS-11 rate and another two to get him back to the Blue River District as ranger. When asked later how he got those jobs, he told me that, in those days, "when vacancies opened up, they looked at these rosters and . . . matched you with a job." You didn't apply. They just called you and said "here's where you're going," just like the military.[7] His next jobs were on the Willamette National Forest, first as assistant for fire and recreation at Oakridge and then as district ranger on the Blue River Ranger District. That experience led him to become deputy forest supervisor on the Mount Hood National Forest and then forest supervisor on the Coconino National Forest in Arizona. By 1980, he had come full circle—back to the Willamette as forest supervisor, where he stayed until he retired. I met him just as he was pondering his exit. He wanted that forest plan finished before leaving.

I was nervous and conscious of time, but after some small talk I moved quickly to my purpose. I had worn one of my power suits for strength and confidence, and it worked. I stayed calm on the outside. I told both men I had heard about Jerry's retirement: "I am very interested in the upcoming forest information officer position," I said. "I've reviewed the Willamette's draft forest plan. I've researched all of you on the leadership team and I know the issues front and back." I had been thinking long and hard about how to get on the Willamette, and I gave them my proposal. "When you announce the public affairs officer position, I would like to apply for the job. I am a little worried that I won't make the cert [the certification for potential employment], so I'm here to tell you why I am the best person for the job." They listened quietly.

My work at the WO had connected me with the Resource Planning Act, I said. I understood agency dealings with its replacement, the National Forest Management Act of 1976. By then, NFMA had become a sort of bible for forest management standards in all national forests and grasslands. NFMA directed the agency to regularly report on the status and trends of renewable resources on forest and grasslands and set a planning standard to guide the Forest Service into the next century. The agency completed its first national forest plans in 1983, and all national forests had to put plans in place by 1990. The deadline loomed. The law also required updating the plans every ten years.[8]

The Willamette had not yet released its first plan and was running up against the clock. I knew that, and so I told them I saw ways to improve the draft plan through better communications, internally and externally, and working closely with the districts to provide input on the final forest plan. "If you hire me, you will get your plan published," I promised. "I know how to build a strong public affairs unit. I won't spend any money for travel, and I only want two things in return: a sabbatical to attend Oregon State University and qualify as forester, and a deputy assignment, understudy to one of your rangers." They smiled and told me they looked forward to receiving my application. I said thank you and left the office, unsurprised by the look of disbelief on their faces, but satisfied with my performance. I headed to Jerry's office.

Complexities of the Willamette

I was glad I had brought my boots along with my power suit that day, because Jerry volunteered to take me out into the forest. First, we headed to Cougar Hot Springs on the Blue River Ranger District. Lynn Burdett was ranger there, and, per standard protocol, Jerry called to let her know we would be on the district. As we got out of Jerry's government car, the spiritually cleansing forest air hit me. We strolled into the lush green of old growth, downed trees, lichen and moss everywhere I looked. Beautiful wildflowers and ferns skipped across the ground in an array of colors. On our walk to the hot springs, I told Jerry I was interested in his job and that I had come to the forest to talk to Mike Kerrick. We moved along quietly, alternating conversation with contemplation, but when we reached the hot springs, the serenity jumped right out of my body. Jerry hadn't told me that some of the people there would be naked! Nudity seemed to have no effect on him. I, on the other hand, tried not to see what was in front of me.

Jerry smiled and said, "Since you wanted me to share some of the issues happening on the forest, I decided to start with Cougar Hot Springs." Jerry and I had never met, but he was a gracious host and had the kind of job I wanted, forest information officer. I had heard about the

Cougar Reservoir and was glad to see it in person. It had been a sore spot in forest administration for years. According to Jerry, the issues included homeless people coming from Eugene getting naked and doing drugs. The problem wasn't nudity. Trashing the hot springs with bottles and needles from drunken, noisy, parties did not go over well with the locals, and also meant that others stayed away from Cougar. We did not stay long; these were the "sexiest" of the Willamette's problems, but Jerry also updated me on other pressing issues, including the use of herbicides.

After clear-cuts, workers sprayed to prevent weeds taking over while they planted. But the chemicals used to remove vegetation were causing members of the Hoedads Cooperative, a group of contracted tree planters, many of them female, to become ill. Research indicated that herbicide use could contribute to miscarriages, and although not conclusive, the possibility concerned forest leadership, as did potential effects on wildlife and water systems. In 1976, the Hoedads and two other organizations had sued the Siuslaw National Forest for an inadequate EIS that did not account for the toxicity of several chemicals, especially phenoxy herbicides. The suit resulted in an injunction on the Siuslaw on spraying herbicides, including TCDD-contaminated herbicides 2, 4, 5-T (2, 4, 5-trichlorophenoxyacetic acid) and Silvex. Another controversial EIS followed in 1981, with a 1983 lawsuit resulting in an injunction against the entire Forest Service, the Bureau of Land Management (BLM), and the Environmental Protection Agency (EPA). None of them could spray until a worst-case analysis had been completed. The draft EIS published in 1987 made this a hot topic, alongside the infamous spotted owl issue that complicated forest management.[9]

We left the hot springs and headed out Highway 58 to the Oakridge Ranger District. Jerry called District Ranger Bob Barsted for suggestions on where we should go. Bob suggested walking the path to Salt Creek Falls, the second-highest waterfall in Oregon. Silence, a fresh, wet, clean smell, and ancient trees met us in a magnificent old-growth forest. Only the call of birds interrupted the crunching leaves as our boots clomped along the path. Then a rushing sound blasted the stillness. It quickly became louder, interrupting my reverie. The intrusion was worth it—I had never seen a waterfall up close before. As I watched cascades of crystal sparkling water with a drifting mist that moved calmly past me, I marveled that nature had created this magical place. I felt like melting into the moss-covered hillside and letting my worries dissipate into the earth. Jerry bragged that this was the second-highest waterfall in Oregon. He said Multnomah Falls was the highest. I made a mental note: *I have to take the kids to see Multnomah Falls.* As we left, the sun cast a beautiful rainbow. Who could say it was not just for me? I pretended it was, and that it predicted a beautiful future.

Riding my trail horse, Smokey, in the Los Padres National Forest.

At Karnowsky Creek in the Siuslaw National Forest.

On field trips.

On my first visit to a ranger station.

Graduation day, University of
Maryland 1985.

On machine duty as acting district ranger at the Silver Lake Ranger District.

Tom Hamilton, my mentor, threw a going-away party.

With Forest Service chief Mike Dombeck during a visit to Mount St. Helens National Monument.

Governor Barbara Roberts of Oregon and me on a grazing and weeds field trip, July 16, 1993, Siuslaw National Forest.

Rafting down the Rogue River.

Skiing on Mount Hood.

Mount St. Helens back-country monitoring trip.

Identifying flora in the
Siuslaw National Forest.

Canopy Crane Show-Me
Trip, Mount Adams, 1998.

Gloria and my son, Andre, at a Historic Oregon Trail Interpretive Center reenactment.

A photo taken at the National Historic Oregon Trail Interpretive Center while I was area manager for the Bureau of Land Management.

Riding the trail on the Los Padres.

Family photo, summer 2019. Front, l to r: Eugene (son-in-law), Phil (partner), me.
Back, l to r: Catrina (daughter), Victoria (granddaughter), Alana (granddaughter), Camille
(daughter), Nyeelah (granddaughter), Andre (son), Nichole (daughter-in-law),
Andre Jr. (grandson).

CHAPTER 4

Awakening the Forester Within

I HEADED BACK TO PORTLAND FEELING GOOD about my time on the Willamette. By late summer, the forest had advertised the public affairs officer job, and when the offer came, it was crying time again. *What should I do?* My son was a senior at Lincoln High School, and although the girls wanted to move out, they all still needed me. I was on my way to an empty nest too soon. I wasn't ready! I hadn't expected to deal with a permanent separation from my children yet.

It was time to get in my car, blast the music, and head for the beach—to think—alone. My emotional state has always related to music, reflecting my moods and challenges and lifting me with the poetry of song. When my husband died, gospel music sustained me. In Montana, I listened to country music with stories of family, home, and romance, alongside soul and R&B. From childhood, I would write down the lyrics from Willie Nelson, along with the words of Aretha Franklin. I had always liked country music, too, even when it wasn't cool. In Montana, everyone liked country, but I never heard soul music on the radio.

That day, as I drove to Yachats, Oregon, I listened to Otis Redding's *Sitting on the Dock of the Bay*, a song about life and the passage of time. That song marks my memory of sitting on the beach, crying, and praying about my future, my children, and the job in Eugene. I knew that the kids would not come with me and I could not stay with them, a realization that reignited the pain of earlier losses. In our society, parents and children separate. I knew that, but logical thinking doesn't mediate emotional anguish. I searched for the stoic, tough woman I had become, trying to find alternatives, but she was hard to locate. I remember the ocean roaring as the tide came in, my stomach deeply knotted like the twisted roots of an old-growth tree. As I contemplated leaving my children alone in Portland, I found myself talking to my dead husband, sobbing until his spirit—and the sea—removed my pain. When the tide went out, I released my torment into the deep, feeling cleansed and reveling in the beautiful Northwest sunset. I knew what I had to do.

On the way home, I listened to Whitney Houston's "Greatest Love of All" and thought about my children and my life. The song reminded me that the greatest love of all is inside yourself. I had been teaching my children all I knew. I had always surrounded them with love, because I knew that was what they needed. I now realized I could rely on myself to make the right choice. In Montana, I had been led to a lonely place but found my strength in love for my children. There's no way I would make the wrong decision for them. I had come to depend on myself, just like the song said. It hadn't been easy.

Sometimes I really missed the support of my extended family, my church, and the friends who knew us well. The little things that helped had disappeared. My parents had never given me money to live on when we were in DC, but they had helped financially now and then, through gift-giving on birthdays and Christmas. After I left home, they sent cards to the children, along with a little money (maybe ten dollars), but no gifts. Before long, the cards stopped coming. It seemed out of sight was out of mind.

Most importantly, my family had helped create happy memories and take the emotional burden from me after Willie James died. In those days, long-distance phone calls were expensive, so we rarely talked with family and friends from back home. I had missed the kinds of conversations that made me feel less alone in raising my children. I had no one to share with about everyday issues or decisions and had learned to rely on myself for counsel. But making this kind of major decision alone was different. I realized I didn't have a single friend to talk with about my deep-seated fears over my emptying nest.

I still had the children, though, and my time on the beach reminded me of our bond. Our family relied on one another and treasured our closeness. We listened to each other, so I called them, said I was on my way home, and to be ready for a family meeting. I asked Andre to think about staying with his best friend, Jerome Persons. I then called Mrs. Persons to see if the family had room for Andre to stay for his twelfth-grade year. I knew that Catrina wanted to move into her own apartment and attend Portland State University, and Nicki wanted to leave college. I asked them to put together a budget for room and board based on where they might be living.

It had been financially difficult for us since the day I lost my husband. Social Security benefits had helped, but in 1982 President Reagan changed the regulations and made it more difficult for the children of single parents (mostly mothers) to get a leg up in the world. Before then, if children went straight to college, they continued to receive Social Security. Reagan's regulations cut benefits at age sixteen, which means household incomes dropped just as kids became even more expensive, with driving and insurance, clothes, proms, and other things, not to mention making it harder to help these kids get a college education. My household was no different.

All I could think was, *Here I go.* I would go back to robbing Peter to pay Paul while I supported more than one household. I was worried about money, but I knew we would figure it out together, as a family—and we did. Trina could get a student loan and live with a friend on Vancouver Avenue in Northeast Portland. Nicki left PCC to work full time for Nordstrom and lived in a one-bedroom apartment on Broadway, so she could walk to work. I still had a heavy financial burden, but the promotion to GS-13 would help. Still, between supporting them and myself, airplane tickets to Washington, DC, to see my family were out of reach. I had to hope for details to the WO—those temporary assignments that often provided additional staff from a forest, when needed, or experience for advancement—if I wanted to see my family again.

On the Willamette

It had taken fifteen and a half years, but I had finally arrived! I knew this was it. The job on the Willamette was the pass through to bigger and better things. I'd known that working on this forest was a key component to my advancement since my time in the WO, where I often met employees detailed there for national office recognition. I had heard from them about the Willamette before I moved to the Northwest. I had also done my research. Have a plan folks—it sure did work for me! I was hell-bent on getting to this major forest for the same reason as the guys: we all wanted to move up!

The Willamette National Forest is more than 1.65 million acres of gorgeous and varied landscape, filled with cool mountain streams, wooded slopes and canyons, and eight wilderness areas—nearly 381,000 acres of backwoods land. The Willamette is both a timber boon and a recreational godsend because of its proximity to cities like Salem, Albany, and Eugene. It includes scenic byways; more than 375 lakes; fifteen hundred miles of rivers and streams, including the headwaters of the McKenzie, Santiam, and Willamette Rivers; and six thousand miles of roads that allow access deep into the forest. Although Douglas-fir is the most common tree, with some old-growth stands still present, conifers like cedar, pine, and hemlock shape a biologically diverse environment. The Willamette hosts more than three hundred species of wildlife and fish, from the northern spotted owl to kokanee (sockeye) salmon, and big game animals like Roosevelt elk and black bear. Several of these species are threatened, and by the time I arrived, supporters of the spotted owl and marbled murrelet had already been making trouble for the Forest Service.[1]

Because of its size, massive timber revenues, and old-school management, the Willamette National Forest regularly turned out employees who were on the rise. Stories about the Willamette forest sat at the heart of the most critical issues faced by the agency during the 1990s. Not only was there money there, but the Willamette also had the kind of leadership that ensured employee development and supported workers with a wide range of training opportunities. I had also learned that Mike Kerrick was the key to that advancement. If you had ambition, he would do what you needed so you could get where you wanted. Because of his mentoring, the Willamette produced rangers, forest supervisors, regional office staffers, regional foresters, WO staff people, and even deputy chiefs. No wonder so many employees wanted to work there!

Kerrick could make opportunities available because the Willamette's budget supported whatever was needed to move up. The forest's nearness to Portland and full staffing also meant money for training. For example, Chuck DeRidder (the regional HR training coordinator) took employees to visit major companies like Google. He also organized a trip to New Mexico to learn about the rich history and different forestry practices in that area. I really wanted to go on that trip! But I'd told Mike when I took the job that I would not leave the forest for any training, so I didn't even ask. I was determined to get that forest plan completed, so that I could qualify as a forester and become a line officer as soon as possible!

I hit the ground running, immediately becoming the voice for my supervisor and talking with the media about a host of issues, such as herbicides, recreation, and other forest controversies. I was in the thick of Forest Service administration, and I loved it. I was proud and knew my family felt the same way. When I saw myself quoted in the paper, I'd underline the statement and send the article to my mom. There was so much to do and learn!

I had never had my own office before, let alone one with a door. I felt pumped! I realized right away that I had a great group of people working for me, with diverse skills. There was Pattie Rogers, information specialist; and Lorette Ray, information technician; and Irene Stumpf, our graphic artist. I got together with the three of them right away to create our annual workplan. As a government bureaucracy, we did not randomly decide what to do. We got our marching orders from the WO, which provided a blueprint for our goals and objectives. We quickly realized that my goal—to complete the mandated forest plan as quickly as possible—meant an aggressive agenda. My staff agreed that we needed another specialist to help accomplish the goals for our public affairs program, which related to national objectives such as sustainable forests. The management team relented, and we got our information specialist. That new hire left me free to focus on finishing the forest plan that had been in the works for approximately ten years by then.

I also became part of the management team, a group that included six rangers (two women and four men) and six staff officers for different areas (recreation, timber, planning, fire, engineering, and public affairs). All the staff officers, except me, were men. Everyone on the leadership team, except me, was white. You might wonder why this race and gender breakdown matters. It's simple. This group, like other management teams around the country, made up the promotable pool for advanced leadership. It was 1990, and this demographic breakdown on a forest known for promotions shows just how unusual it was for me, a black woman, to be in this position. I knew that then, and I marvel at it now.

Forest Supervisor Mike Kerrick led the team, with Deputy Mike Edrington rounding out our monthly meeting. I was finally part of the group that made important decisions, and for the first time my voice mattered. Joe Mancuso, our personnel officer, also had a regular seat at the table. As the main union contact, he came to our meetings to discuss staffing and disciplinary issues with the management team.[2] Mike ran focused, coordinated, and sometimes facilitated meetings, and everyone communicated clearly. Forests and districts sometimes presented at these meetings, giving employees rare face-to-face time that provided them opportunity to share their experiences and gave us a chance to assess their skills. We also looked at projects and landscapes "on the ground." As in Montana, these experiences provided valuable team-building opportunities.

One time, we went on a camping trip that Mike announced we'd better not miss, short of a death in the family. I decided that if I wanted to be a real forester—and I did—I needed my own camping equipment, but what to buy?! So, I went to REI and queried one of the store clerks. He wanted to know if I was camping in a park, at a campsite in the woods, or in a wilderness. *So many details,* I thought, *I just want to go camping!* I was overwhelmed by all of the "stuff" everywhere: canoes hanging from the ceiling; tents up on shelves; and plenty of things I couldn't even name. I didn't say any of that out loud, though. One of my key management qualities is that I am a big-picture person. I know how to delegate when necessary, and I put this skill into practice, both in my job and my life.

I politely told him that I would be camping in the national forest with my management team. I had no idea what I needed. So the clerk picked out my tent, found me the right kind of sleeping bag, and told me I'd need a canteen, flashlight, and gun. Just kidding about the gun! The rest is true. A lot of folks had guns in the woods, but I wasn't one of them. I got hiking boots, socks and moleskin to protect my feet from blisters, and bug spray. My in-store helper made sure I bought everything I needed and more, and boy did he make a killing off of me! He even tried to sell me a disposable wilderness toilet, but I said "No, no, no." I could deal with bathroom issues like everyone else. I did appreciate his reminder to take toilet tissue. I still smile as I remember telling my family about these experiences over the course of my career and all the gear I bought for camping, rafting, golfing, hiking, skiing, and even fishing. None of them had ever done these kinds of activities, and they jokingly asked if I had any money left for food.

Mike picked a place for our trip near Opal Creek Wilderness, a site of controversy in the 1980s over plans to cut old growth. Opal Creek is one of those places where peace reigns in the stillness of gigantic trees, the burble of creeks, and the occasional tap-tapping of a woodpecker breaking through the silence. We found a nice high spot near a river with a great view of the steep ridges of the Bull of the Woods Wilderness. That night Mike cooked and we sat around a campfire eating and telling stories. Most of them talked about times on the ground—in the field, as we say. I could not compete with those stories, but I could talk about the WO. You can bet I didn't mention all that I knew about people who worked in DC, though I could have told some doozies!

The Washington office had been my wilderness. I knew it up and down, back and front. When people went there for the first time, they'd feel like I did in the woods—unsettled, unclear, and excited. We stayed in the woods the entire weekend, and I left knowing that our team was stronger for getting to know one another. We had all learned a lot, and I now felt I belonged. Unlike Montana, this time when I shared that I wanted to be a ranger, nobody laughed.

The Willamette Forest Plan

After our camping trip, everyone got busy working on the forest plan. Nationwide, most forests had completed their plans, but ours lagged. Forest plans set overall management guidance at the forest level, rather than by district, and they had to be completed every fifteen years.[3] We use the plans to identify specific use areas, ranging from timber harvests to protecting rare plants and primitive recreation areas; to determine where motorized vehicles or snowmobiles can go; to designate whether trails are for horses or for walking only; and to balance multiple-use mandates with sustainable resource use to maintain healthy ecosystems.[4] The Willamette staff had been working on its plan for nearly ten years under the 1982 Planning Rule. The rule required public participation after a draft plan had been developed and during the environmental analysis process required by the National Environmental Policy Act (NEPA). Things have since changed. Now, the public, including state and tribal groups and community members, are involved in developing plans, but then the public primarily reviewed plans after the fact and then weighed in.[5]

Comprehensive forest planning was convoluted, complicated, and iterative.[6] We had to approach the land as one unit, which meant district planning came first. This planning required public interaction, and preparation by the management team of alternatives for how much timber to cut, the activities allowed on recreation sites and their locations, wilderness activity, and so forth. The dichotomy between timber and other forest needs is why I went into the field: to find out just how viable the levels of timber production were compared with what happened on the ground. Rolf Anderson, as the staff planning officer, was always frontline in all planning discussions.

We don't build alternatives in a vacuum, and districts don't operate in silos. Feedback affects the entire forest, which means that plans need to be published collectively, because the land itself exists as an ecological whole. District rangers did the analysis, and if something changed on a nearby district, they might have to do it all over again. After districts revised their plans based on public comments and input from specialists, we compiled this information for the final product. NEPA often required environmental impact statements or environmental assessments before project implementation. We used this process both before and after publishing the forest plans. Our current job was to ferret out the many possibilities, so that Mike could pick the "preferred alternative."

My staff and I took field trips to ranger stations to see ongoing district work and talk about options. I recall sensing a small amount of competition and a large amount of pride during these visits, along with mutual respect. Although a lot of work had been completed, I still had to sit in on public meetings, as each district presented alternatives based on models from their own land base. They would present four or five alternatives to the public as they came out of the initial process, and we organized the information into a draft plan for citizen feedback. By the time I arrived, most districts had already presented their drafts, and comments poured in to the supervisor's office (SO), where my staff compiled the data, received the mail, wrote responses, and prepared briefing books for public presentation. We assembled this information from ranger districts to create a holistic plan. My job was to listen, sometimes facilitate, and supervise pulling the information together into an EIS for final public review and publishing.

Public affairs was involved at the district and SO levels, so I spent a lot of time at these meetings. I wanted people to feel they had been heard, so my staff captured the comments and documented the issues empirically. When we talked about herbicides, Irene, a photographer and illustrator, took pictures of the affected land. Those pictures became part of the materials used for evaluation and public demonstration. Because my staff and I presented the public face of the forest, we all had to be knowledgeable about forest issues.

Determining the preferred alternatives relied on a computer program called FORPLAN that allowed planners to break forests into zones based on geography, wildlife, roads, water, and use data to determine outputs, like how much timber to cut for maximum profit. An Oregon State University professor, Norm Johnson, had created the computer model, and it became the primary analysis tool for Forest Service land management planning as the agency inventoried forests nationwide in the 1980s and 1990s. FORPLAN was far more sophisticated than earlier methods, because planners could test alternatives—for more or less cutting, harvests nearer or closer to the water, and the effects on different types of nearby recreational sites.[7] The national forests were required to use it, but, boy did I hear a lot of complaints about FORPLAN! The computer model was supposed to spit out preferred alternatives that included all kinds of possibilities, not just for timber, but no one really knew how to use it well. Nor could FORPLAN evaluate how attitudes or emotions would play into decision making. Eventually, the agency turned to other models, but FORPLAN remains legendary to those who struggled with it!

I was always concerned about the numbers for proposed timber sales on the Willamette. When I first read the draft plan, I knew our numbers—from 550 to 600 million board feet (mmbf)—were too high, especially given a new emphasis on forest health. Public feedback made clear that however we used the model, it didn't reflect the real effects of timber harvests. The premise was wrong, and none of the alternatives were sustainable. I found it interesting that all that work on alternatives in the forest planning process did little in the moment to help with current activities like managing wildlife habitat, roadless areas, or fish and recreation, among other activities. There's real time, and there's final forest plan time. The computer model outputs did not help the rangers with work on the ground. It was all about projections. District work plans would not change until the final plan was in place, and practices remained the same during the ten-year planning process.

Foresters, "Ologists," and Activism

The good news was that I had finally made it to the Willamette, the forest of advancement. Unfortunately, a decade of conflict among loggers, environmentalists, politicians, journalists, the public, and even our own employees had created a tumultuous environment. By the time I joined the Willamette, more and more employees with environmental leanings worked for the Forest Service. These were the "ologists," who joined the agency in the 1970s and were increasingly important to fulfilling environmental mandates. By 1990, nearly two decades of university programs had included more than silviculture. Even forestry programs had courses on watershed management and policies related to the clean air and water acts. The law, educational changes, and a transforming workforce shifted employees' views of our activities from pride about harvesting efficiency to concern over practices. This brings me to Jeff DeBonis, a Willamette employee with a degree in forest management. Jeff had worked as a forester for the agency since 1978, but became part of the new guard in the Forest Service, people who felt more strongly about ecosystems than about tree harvests. Many of these newer employees saw our mission differently than had earlier foresters, which resulted in nationwide internal conflict. Jeff brought that strife into the public eye.

In 1990, DeBonis created an organization called the Association of Forest Service Employees for Environmental Ethics (AFSEEE). He pointed to what he called the "agency's willful violation of the spirit and intent of environmental laws, which was causing extensive overcutting and damage to our national forests."[8] AFSEEE tried to hold the Forest Service accountable by exposing its actions to the public through a newsletter, while facilitating lawsuits to halt timber sales. The newsletter informed agency employees and hundreds of citizen supporters about timber sales and recreation and other policy decisions that sometimes ignored environmental laws. Every ranger district in the nation received the newsletter, as did anyone else who joined AFSEEE. Many saw DeBonis as a troublemaker. Others thought him a hero, especially if they shared his environmental ideals. That's why he started AFSEEE in the first place, to give a voice to that group of people.

Mike was the only person in the Forest Service to deal with a situation like this, with an internal employee speaking so publicly against the agency. We weren't sure how to proceed. Joe Mancuso handled all personnel issues, and he researched whether the forest had any legal liability related to Jeff. We both worked with Supervisor Kerrick and the union to understand Jeff's rights as an employee. Could he be fired for spreading messages contrary to our actions but in keeping with environmental law? We were in uncharted territory. The year before (1989), a Whistleblower Protection Act had reinforced the power of federal employees to report wrongdoing in government—and DeBonis was a whistleblower. Employees have the right, and some say the obligation, to report agency misconduct to the Office of Special Counsel if there is a violation of a law or regulation, mismanagement, wasting of funds, an abuse of authority, or a threat to public health or safety.[9] But this seemed different, or was it? DeBonis did more than report the agency to its bosses. He aired our dirty laundry in public.

The RO and WO were very interested in our situation, which placed me right in the middle. As the public affairs officer and the voice for the forest, I had to carry my boss's message to the outside world. Internally, we asked, *What are we going to do about this guy?* I admired Jeff for speaking out, but he presented a problem for the forest and for me. My admiration had to be pushed aside. I had to think, instead, about how to manage the press surrounding this employee who promoted actions contrary to our goals. We had to find a way to move forward that would satisfy timber interests and everyone else—that was my main focus.

Fortunately, at some point, Jeff began to think he could do more from outside than inside the organization, and he left the Forest Service. Jeff's shift in loyalty, from the agency's conservation ideals to environmental ethics, caused major disruption in the Forest Service of the 1990s. But, while many people could—and do—critique his methods for bringing awareness to activities, the organization he founded lives on. AFSEEE now boasts more than one thousand members, mostly current and former

FS employees. Today, Forest Service employees don't have to hide their AFSEEE newsletter in a brown paper bag anymore. Up-to-date information about the environment and government ethics is now available on a website for all the world to see.[10] Jeff's actions took courage.

The Willamette was a hotbed of conflict in a lot of other ways, too, especially as demands among forest users came to a boiling point. Externally, we had environmentalists chaining themselves to trees at timber sales and organizing protests outside the federal building in downtown Portland. These situations forced us to involve the police to establish order, and because I handled communications, I became the voice between environmentalists and the Forest Service. One day, environmental activists chained themselves to Mike's desk to protest timber harvests. Mike wasn't there, because I had suggested he leave, which is how I ended up in the middle of it. In those days, you could just walk into any government office. Now you're screened and checked for guns when entering a federal building. But then, I had to deal with this small group of young angry activists. I remember my family and friends back east could hardly believe what was going on out here. They listened intently to my stories about spotted owls and clear-cuts, the practice by which the Forest Service removed all the trees from large parcels of land, wiping the forest clean, while leaving slash behind. I bent their ears about my forest plan work, educated them about losing salmon habitat, following the rules, and the dangers of herbicides.

I don't recall questioning our mission at that point, because whatever my beliefs while I worked in public affairs, I pushed them aside. To tell the truth, I really didn't think about my own position on these issues. I do remember feeling that the protesters went too far when people started chaining themselves to trees and dangerously placing bolts into trees. I'm now aware that my environmental ethics began to emerge out of those experiences, but not to the point that I felt conflicted. I knew that my personal feelings weren't relevant to the job. Later, when I became a leader who determined what happened on the ground, I would bring my environmental principles into play.

These were just a few of the issues facing me as the public affairs officer for the Willamette National Forest. Yet, every day on the Willamette also presented opportunities to learn something new, to engage in historic, important on-the-ground projects. This became a time of huge professional growth, and I remained very satisfied with my decision to come to the Willamette. I hadn't talked much about the forest itself in DC, so I was learning all the time, figuring out more about my own thinking every time I called my mom and had to explain things to her. She didn't know about wilderness, riparian zones, why people would chain themselves to trees, how a bird could be so important—none of the things I'd learned over the years. My education was fluid, and I reinforced it by talking to my family. My city family and friends told me it sounded like I spoke a foreign language. They were right. I explained that I *was* speaking another language, a Pacific Northwest environmental dialect that was becoming second nature.

Completing the Forest Plan

The Willamette National Forest took satisfaction in the amount of timber it sold. In 1989, Region 6 held nearly sixty thousand timber sales and harvested more than five million board feet of timber.[11] According to Mike Kerrick, the Willamette held 15 percent of those sales and harvested about 12 percent of the region's total, close to 650,000 board feet of timber. We all knew that timber sales provided jobs for industry and money for rural communities. The motto of "the greatest good for the greatest number" fueled the Willamette, and we took pride in that motto. Our team knew that timber harvests had already come *way* down, and we needed to reduce the cut further to meet forest plan goals. We also knew that management would not agree to the harvest numbers that came out of FORPLAN, calculations that included leaving what the wildlife biologist, hydrologist, and fish biologist deemed necessary for spotted owls and salmon to thrive. The "ologists" considered preserving riparian areas and halting clear-cutting critical. This would change everything.

As we neared completion of the forest plan, my thoughts turned to how quickly I could move to the next level. First, Rolf and I had to complete my last big job as public affairs officer on the Willamette—organizing a forest-wide leadership meeting that tested my facilitation skills. The forest management team, all the district rangers, and their management teams came together for a precedent-setting discussion. We had to go from draft to final forest plan. Just what did we need? How could we meet environmental mandates and maintain our forest's reputation and economic position? Everyone knew that continued high harvest levels would not sit well with the public. We had to reduce the allowable cut, and as meeting facilitator I pushed hard for the numbers to come down.

I remember the tone of the room at the Eugene Hilton when the forest's line officers and staff heard the final proposal. Tensions were high. But this was a professional meeting, and everyone understood that we must identify a preferred alternative harvest number lower than the numbers in the draft. The leadership team had to think differently than ever before. Our preferred alternative reduced timber production by almost half; management liked the maximum-production-of-timber alternative, even though the numbers were unsustainable. Rolf knew the final number was too high, but by agreeing, we finally got our plan published. Rolf Anderson, our planning staff, and the management team successfully produced the final plan in 1989. For the first time, environmentalists and the timber industry saw harvest reductions. Soon after, Mike Kerrick retired. It all seemed too much for him; he had been in charge of one of the most vibrant, productive national forests in the country. We were also going through workforce reductions, with nearly half the Region 6 workforce eliminated or transferred between 1987 and 2010.[12] Mike had overseen the final days of massive timber harvests. These declining harvests and "downsizing" meant that nothing would ever be the same.

Before Mike's last day on the forest, he kept his promise to me. Mike, Joe Mancuso, and I put together a sabbatical so that I could attend Oregon State University in Corvallis. As one of his final acts, Mike, a person truly instrumental in my career, signed the necessary paperwork to send me to school. I would finally move from a female-dominated administrative position to a male-dominated profession. I would be a forester now!

A new forest supervisor could have made a different choice and changed the trajectory of my career and life, so I am forever grateful to Mike. I had loved living in Eugene. The diversity of people, the farmers market, all the activities around the Willamette River, and so much more. Now I had to find a place in Corvallis and start forestry certification at Oregon State University. I was forty-four years old, not only a returning woman student, but also an ambitious Forest Service employee and one of very few African Americans to attend the program. I needed enough credits to qualify as a forester by US classification standards. That would be the only way to really move up in the agency, something I had known for a long time. As for Mike and his wife Sue, we remain friends for life.

OSU and Peavy Hall

Corvallis looked to me like a Norman Rockwell painting and was considerably less diverse than Eugene. It also reminded me of my first surprising visit to the Pacific Northwest, when I compared the region's population to the snowy white Mount Hood. Some cultural diversity existed, but not much. Corvallis is the classic university town, with many liberal residents who love their environment and their football team, the Beavers. I was more interested in the environment than football, and quickly found pleasure in everything around me. This was my time to connect with the land, go on picnics, bike, hike, and engage in all things outdoors. I loved the wildflowers in the spring and summer as the elevation increased upward to Marys Peak, a site south of Corvallis managed by the Forest Service and, at 4,097 feet, the highest point in the Coast Range. Marys River, a Willamette tributary, provided wonderful habitat for fish and wildlife, and drinking water for Corvallis and Philomath.

I enjoyed walking, and so I got a place about three miles from school. But, one of the best things about Corvallis was meeting my friend, Karen Tressler. Lucky for me, Karen is very outgoing. There is no doubt that I was easy to spot in Peavy Hall, the home of forestry training. I was probably the only African American student there. I am forever grateful that Karen, with her beautiful smile and big brain, sought me out. I never could have imagined, when she first approached me, the role she would play in my life. Karen was a graduate student in the School of Forestry. She knew all the professors, had taken all the courses, and she steered me like a light guides a ship in the fog. I had not been in a classroom for more than a decade, and going back to school was hard!

As a girl, I was the smartest person in the family, better-read even than Mom and Dad, except when it came to the Bible. I would spend hours helping my siblings with their homework, including my sister, who was two grades ahead of me. This academic ease followed me to the University of Maryland, where I maintained a 3.5 GPA, while raising three children and working. But I was younger then, and in retrospect it seemed easy. I still retained the burning desire to learn new things. I had been a journalism major, after all, but forestry presented totally foreign models and concepts. It forced me to grapple with science and math like never before.

Despite more than a decade in the Forest Service, the forestry program was like learning a new language. I found myself wishing I had grown up, like so many employees, in a logging town like Oakridge, Oregon, or Forks, Washington. At least then I might have felt more comfortable with the curriculum. One of my first classes, Dendrology (the scientific study of trees), provides a good example of how Karen handled me. At first, I thought the class would be a piece of cake. After all, I knew trees—I worked for the Forest Service! But I had no idea just how many different types of trees grew in the Pacific Northwest. Wow, there were more than fifty native common broadleaf trees and conifers, each with additional species within the genus!

It got worse. I had to know the scientific names of *all* these trees. Oh my God! There was *Quercus rubra*, red oak; *Quercus garryana*, Oregon white oak; *Quercus kelloggii*, California black oak; and *Quercus chrysolepis*, canyon live oak, just to name a few. I remember thinking, *I'll never use the Latin unless they expect me to take a priest to the forest and impress him with my language skills. Are you kidding me?* That's where Karen came in. Not only did she become my friend, she became one of the most influential people in my life outside the Forest Service. I'm not sure how I would have made it through school without her. Karen helped me academically and socially by connecting me to her network, which included the dean, professors, and a host of friends. Before long, they all became my champions. She was instrumental in my study techniques. We put the Latin words on note cards and she made me walk around campus identifying each tree and saying its Latin name until I had memorized them all. Hey, it worked. I passed the class!

Exams were also hard because there was so much reading. I learn visually, so I had to review my lecture notes over and over again, and Karen made sure I did it. We also joked a lot, which made the learning more fun. I remember telling Karen I could just put all my materials under my pillow to absorb while sleeping, and I would pass. She joked that she'd considered cracking my skull open and dropping in the information I needed to memorize. I'm glad she abandoned that idea and passed on some good study skills instead. She said I was the most difficult student she had ever worked with—because I took so long to study. All of this was new to me, but it was textbook for her. Instructing me was like teaching a first-grader how to read and write. She worked hard! I was devoted, but sadly, studying meant putting a halt to my social life. In Eugene, I regularly went out and had dinner with friends and met people for it's-five-o'clock-somewhere-themed gatherings. Now I had to stay home and study.

Still, when I compared my coursework with my Forest Service work, there was no contest. Yes, OSU was academically challenging, and I can't imagine passing classes with As and Bs without Karen's guidance or my agency experience, but I couldn't imagine quitting either. I *knew* I could get through OSU. I have always known who I am and figured out how to get what I want. At OSU, I had to remind myself of that determination. I had been well on my way to a journalism career. *I could have been just as successful in that field*, I told myself, *because I always do my homework*, whether in school or on the job. *I'm just being tested in a different way. I can do this!*

Professor Rebecca Johnson, later an OSU administrator, became my adviser. Not only did she guide me, but her class was also one of my favorites. We talked about Forest Service, but she moved beyond the rules, regulations, and laws to discuss the tensions between social issues and agency responses. To this day, I remember what I learned from her about the critical role of recreation to Americans' collective psyche. Humans needed to connect with nature for their personal health, and outdoor recreation is imperative to the nation's well-being. I knew Forest Service, but now I understood the differences among the National Park Service, state recreation programs, and other government entities, too. State and federal agencies had different rules, and the Department of Agriculture Forest Service and Department of Interior Park Service had different goals. I would experience some of these differences later in my career.

Dr. George Stankey, sometimes referred to as the "father of wilderness management" also became a good friend and unofficial adviser. Professor Stankey had a good ear for what went on not only inside Peavy Hall, but also inside and outside the Forest Service, in part because he had worked as an agency research social scientist in Montana. Our coffee-time meetings generated food for thought and served as informal tutoring for all my subjects. George, one of the authors of *Wilderness Management*, a 1978 Forest Service publication,[13] could talk for hours about the meaning of wilderness. At the time, universities all over the country used his book, which goes into the history of wilderness and issues surrounding the many fights among the agency, the Wilderness Society, and the public. The critical question asked in this book is, "What is Wilderness?"

From a narrow legal perspective, wilderness is defined as an area possessing qualities outlined in section 2(c) of the Wilderness Act of 1964, "where the earth and its community of life are untrammeled by man." Wilderness is federal land, retains its "primeval character and influence," and is "protected and managed" to "preserve natural conditions." It should be five thousand or more acres, affected "by the forces of nature," not humans, and provide opportunity "for solitude or a primitive and unconfined type of recreation." There may also be valuable resources, "ecological, geological . . . scientific, educational, scenic, or historical."[14]

At the other extreme, wilderness is potentially the entire universe, a philosophical idea rather than a material reality.[15] George's stories and our impromptu discussions did not call for tests at the end. Thank goodness, because I felt like a starving starstruck fan gorging on everything he said. He was also funny, telling us he would advise newbie forest supervisors for his regular contract price. I know George was probably joking, but later I called on him for expert advice regarding a wilderness decision on the Los Padres. He did not charge me for his time, but I did pay his airfare. After I left OSU, George, Karen, and I remained good friends, and I sometimes saw him at show-me trips on the Willamette.

I had a lot of new experiences at OSU. A palpable electricity came from young people on the brink of new lives, and peace washed over me as I walked the campus alone or hiked in the McDonald-Dunn Forest. I felt the camaraderie of new friendships and the thrill of possibility. Sometimes I felt like a fresh, excited college student; other times, I was reminded of being a professional Forest Service employee and a mother. An experience with my study partner, Jeffrey Owens from Halfway, Oregon, reminds me of the vague status that came with being a returning woman student. Jeffrey was young and tall, with blue-green eyes in an oval face, dark thick eyebrows, and a rugged look that reminded me of cowboys I'd seen on TV. Although shy at first, he made me laugh with his farm jokes and feel maternal as he talked about the ranch where he grew up and his dreams for the future. Jeffrey had been only twelve when his mother died, and he reminded me of my college-age son. The two of us studied together once a week for two months. He was an effective partner, who often came to our sessions with the chapter outlined and the questions and answers likely for a pop quiz. I enjoyed his bright young mind and connecting over the material. We even started going out for beer and pizza after our study sessions.

I remember thinking Jeffrey looked *good* in his Stetson hat and pointed-toe leather cowboy boots, but I never thought of him as a romantic possibility. He, apparently, thought otherwise. One night, Jeffrey declared his feelings. He wanted to know if we "maybe could start dating" and said he could tell that I liked being around him, which was true, but I was shocked. I was having fun, but I swear I never saw it coming!

"I'm old enough to be your mother," I told him. He answered by leaning across the table and giving me a peck on the lips in front of God and everyone at the pizza shop. I was so embarrassed! Here I was with a boy my son's age—and he had just kissed me. And he was white! I was completely taken aback. It was the first time I realized what was going on. I had unintentionally stepped over that motherly boundary. I looked around and no one seemed to care about Jeffrey's open display of affection, except me. I gently took each of his hands in mine and told him how sweet he was. "I'm sorry if I've done anything to lead you down this path," I said, "but we can never have a relationship."

He looked at me with his blue-green eyes, tilted his head and asked, "How did you feel when I kissed you?" Inside I had a few butterflies, but I told him, "I never meant to lead you on." He was visibly disappointed, especially when I said we needed to end our study sessions for good. We stayed for a while longer, talking until we felt comfortable enough to say goodnight; as I walked home, I considered the kiss. I felt both guilty and pleased that a beautiful young man had admired me. I was in my early fifties, so, not past romance, but I was no Mrs. Robinson! Karen was my only study partner after that.

I'm a Forester Now!

I got through OSU with good grades, a lifetime friend, and a tremendous sense of accomplishment. I enjoyed the sense of pride that comes with knowledge and the freedom that came with not having to work daily from 9:00 a.m. till 5:00 p.m. or longer. The day I returned to the Willamette, Joe

Mancuso prepared the paperwork that moved me from an administrative professional, 1082 Public Affairs Specialist series, to a Management 460 Forester series, a shift comparable to the difference between a noncommissioned and a commissioned officer—a sergeant versus a lieutenant. Joe also presented my new assignment. I would be an assistant ranger on the Rigdon Ranger District under the tutelage and supervision of Ranger Herb Wick. Herb and I had worked together on the management team, and I suspect he looked forward to the challenge of turning me into a forester. "One more thing," Joe said, "The district is over fifty miles away. We will move you up there if that's where you want to live." I definitely wanted to go. A real forester doesn't live in the city if it's possible to live near the woods. I was finally going to a ranger district office, this one in Westfir, Oregon, one of more than six hundred districts in the country. This is where the forester's work happens. I wish I could have stayed there forever.

Small towns like Westfir are the real heart of the Forest Service, and a few statistics show just how unusual it is for people of color to live and work in them, and how alone they are when they do. According to the census, in 1931 Westfir boasted a population of five hundred. By the time I got there in the early 1990s, the population was around 278. It dropped to 253 by 2010, with one lone African American listed; I wouldn't be surprised if that person worked for the Forest Service. I was pushing against the tide in 1990. Even now, the numbers show just how hard it still is for people of color to work for the agency. The nearby town of Oakridge, where I lived, had just over three thousand people in 1990 and was not very diverse. In 2010, still only thirty-one African Americans lived in Oakridge, a jump from the fourteen counted there ten years earlier, but still less than 1 percent of the population.[16]

The ranger district sat in the valley of the Cascade Range, completely surrounded by the Willamette National Forest and about fifty miles east of Eugene. The proximity and easy access via Highway 58 made the area a natural tourist destination. People came to hike, ride mountain bikes, and revel in wildflowers, fishing, and water sports. Nearby Willamette Pass provided a host of winter sports that also operated out of the district. The town of Oakridge tried to use its destination status—ecotourism—to revive itself after the two major failures, first of the railroad and then of the timber economy. The four largest employers were the school district,

Armstrong Wood Products, Oakridge Sand & Gravel, and the Forest Service. Otherwise, the coffee shop or grocery store and a few mom-and-pop businesses were about the only places to get a job. Oakridge had suffered the fate of many small towns and, like them, felt abandoned. The privately owned mills got their timber from the surrounding national forest, but timber production fell in the 1980s, primarily because the old machines could not deal with smaller trees as the old growth disappeared. I was now truly in the mouth of the beast, engrossed "on the ground" in the conflicting issues that played out in the Pacific Northwest. This is where the employees who marked the timber, dumped the garbage, kept the trails clear, maintained the campgrounds, did the firefighting, greeted visitors—and so much more—lived and worked.

My best education about what the Forest Service does—everything from fire to recreation to special use permits to timber—I learned on the Rigdon Ranger District. But, as much as I loved being a district ranger at Rigdon and a citizen of Oakridge, Oregon, as much as I believed I could be happy there for the rest of my life, I knew I couldn't stay. Remember, all forest supervisors live in cities—and that was my goal!

CHAPTER 5

Cattlemen, Cowboys, and the Oregon Trail

MY FIRST DAY ON THE JOB, IN DECEMBER 1991, Ranger Herb Wick called an all-employees meeting. He briefly introduced me as the assistant ranger. "I'm very glad to welcome Gloria," he told the staff, "and I'm sure this place will feel like home to her in no time at all. Join me in welcoming Gloria to our district family." Afterward, he gave me the floor.

I had always liked my breech birth analogy, so I began with that story—how I started in the WO and ended on a district by way of two regional headquarters and a forest supervisor's office. And then I told them, "I went to OSU with the goal of being a forester. It didn't take me long to realize that getting the title would not make me a 'forester,' but that is still my goal. I'm hoping to share what I know with you, and in return I hope you will help me become a better forester as I work for you and beside you." With the end of my speech, and what sounded like sincere applause, we moved to the dining hall, to one of the best potlucks I have ever attended. I hadn't seen such a big spread at a Forest Service gathering before. This smorgasbord could have fed all of us for a week! It seemed like everyone on the district had prepared a dish—and that made me feel good, as if each contribution reflected an individual welcome, as if the communion immediately connected me to the people here. I knew right away that I would really enjoy this place.

I worked my way around the room, talking with lower-level employees, mostly women who seemed happy to see a female line officer. I had been a little anxious, so was relieved when folks told me they were glad I chose their district for my new home. I got questions like, "How soon can we have you over for dinner?" "Can you help me understand why more African Americans don't want to work out here?" and "How does it feel to go from the big city to rural Oakridge?"

I wasn't so sure about the level of acceptance from staff officers. These were the specialists, the foresters and "ologists" who provided expertise to management, especially in planning situations. I didn't sense the same warmth from them as I had with the women employees. These were all men, white men, and I would be in charge of them. Some welcomed me with kind words that did not match their body language and unfriendly side glances. I wondered, *Are these the guys I'll have to work with?*

They were! I quickly realized I would have to really prove myself to earn a place at the staff officer table. I was right. I was at Rigdon for more than two years (until March 1994), and during that time we finally got to the place where they viewed me as a legitimate part of the leadership team, but it took a while.

When the meet-and-greet ended, Herb and I went back to his office. "Gloria," he said, "an assistant ranger is considered number two after the district ranger. Having an assistant ranger used to be common in the Forest Service before I started in the 1970s, but I had not heard these positions were being reactivated until Joe called me about you." I responded by asking Herb how he felt about my assignment. How could I be valuable to him? Did he have work I could take off his hands?

Herb was a traditional ranger with an entirely male staff. A nontraditional ranger would have had a more diverse staff by the mid-1990s, but Herb had the type of autocratic leadership style common for ranger districts. I knew this, and so was extremely happy to hear what he had to say: "I want you to get to know the district, the ground, and the employees," he began, "so that at some point, when you speak to them, they will know it's the same as me talking to them." He continued, "I would like for you to directly supervise the planning team, and every chance you get, I want you to go into the field! Learn about the projects we are doing." Then he said, "This is your chance to earn your stripes. Learn about timber, roads, recreation, and other projects on the ground. Read the environmental assessments and decisions I've signed to see if they match what's happening. You think you're up to this?"

I had been listening intently, and my body showed it. I leaned forward and smiled, my head immediately bobbing up and down to signal compliance. "I am more than up to it!" I was so excited that I wanted to hug him but knew it was totally inappropriate. I had always been a hugger, but now I was in a leadership position, where I was the one with power, and I had to stop. I made a mental note that I should not go around hugging people. I didn't want to be charged with sexual assault.

When I left Herb's office, Bev McCulley, one of the timber presale technicians, was waiting to introduce me to the planning staff and other employees. In retrospect, I realize that I always had at least one special friend to help me navigate through the known and the unknown. Most of these people ended up as friends for life. In Missoula it was Arlen Roll. In the Portland RO it was Barbara Ingersoll. At OSU, I had Karen Tressler. On the Willamette, it was Diana Bus. Now, at Rigdon, Bev McCulley took that role. Bev had always lived in Oakridge and was a pillar of the community. She coached her children's softball team and had a big presence elsewhere in town and at school. Most everyone in Oakridge knew Bev, and we became very good friends. She and I spent time together doing all kinds of things, but one of my favorite memories is going out on the golf course with her. Staff and employees on a district do not usually have our kind of close friendship. The hierarchy typically was ranger, then deputy (the formal title for assistant—me), then staff officers, who interacted with the employees only from a business standpoint. The general rule was to never cross the work/life line. Everything was business and no joking around: *This is a job, no time for smiling. If you're doing the job wrong, I'll tell you. We aren't here to have fun.* That is harder when the employees are your friends, but I knew I could be a professional leader and enjoy my days inside and outside the office. Oakridge was such a small community that I'm sure others on the leadership team had friendships outside the district. But everyone knew that Bev and I were friends. We laughed, we challenged, and we worked hard—together.

Interdisciplinary Work: Resource Planning and Timber

By the 1990s, the Forest Service was promoting self-directed work groups and an open work style. Many found this shift hard. The agency had always been hierarchical, and people expected management to provide clear direction. Under this new work model, we organized ourselves as an integrated resource planning team (IRP). I had never heard this term, or about such a process, in Forest Service before, but I knew about interdisciplinary teams forming around the nation to do the planning work required by NEPA and NFMA. The idea was to meet legal planning requirements and also bring people with different perspectives together for better environmental outcomes.

Before this, a planning team would go to an individual staff member, like the wildlife biologist, to write up that person's piece of the planning document. That person would go to the hydrologist, who weighed in with her expertise. Then came the archaeologist, who wrote up her piece, before all of it went to the planners. The key difference between the IRP approach and the old work model before was that, before, the work happened in silos. With the IRP approach, employees in various disciplines talked face-to-face. This brought staff officers together with specialists to create, understand, and jointly develop land management practices and projects. We now worked together to prepare environmental assessments for projects that ranged from timber sales to trails.

By necessity, IRPs, which began voluntarily, became much more popular—and necessary—as fewer employees were left to do planning in the midst of the reduction in force (commonly called RIF). Our team included foresters and silviculturists, along with staff officers and "ologists" like wildlife biologist Ken Kestner and the hydrologist. There were specialists for recreation and presalers like Bev, John Ager, and Glenna MacKinnon. Together, we used maps to identify planning areas and determine which projects to address. The ranger participated, too, and both of us went out into the field with the appropriate disciplinary team member, to areas with environmental assessments (EAs) in progress. Each discipline and activity had its own protocol. If we looked at a timber sale, our wildlife biologist came along to figure out how to deal with downed wood and determine the sale's effect on rivers, streams, and wildlife. The hydrologist also came, to evaluate the potential for sedimentation and make recommendations. Of course, presale staff was there, too, along with the rest of us.

Everything still revolved around timber, though EAs on the Rigdon District often included other projects. Say you had a timber sale with a thirty-mile radius, and you wanted a trail or a new toilet or a dispersed recreation site within the sale radius—timber money made it possible. That's where presalers came in. They were the timber people, and once a timber EA had been completed, work started on the ground. If recreation staff wanted a trail, presalers decided whether it would work or not. The wildlife biologist determined which trees to keep, and the presalers painted those trees, marked them for commercial sale or wildlife, determined trail placement, and shaped sale boundaries. They did whatever was needed, including landscape preparation. Sometimes that meant working with contractors, supervised by the biologists, to blow the tops off of trees and create snags for spotted owls.

Downsizing and the "Bad Girls"

My friendship with Bev meant that I learned what was really going on with district employees. Sadly, much of what she shared related to employees who were leaving because of the agency's reduction in force. Over time, Region 6 lost approximately one-half of its ten thousand employees. "Downsizing" affected all the regional national forests but hit the districts especially hard. Staff had to find creative ways to do more with less. Between 1991 and 1994 (the time I was there), Rigdon lost 15 percent of its eighty employees. That's a lot of people for a small group. We lost planners, presale people, and members of other critical disciplines that had allowed different groups to work both independently and together.

Despite mutual support, a nervous energy permeated the district office, invisible, but rising and falling like the low-level buzz of saws on a far-off timber sale. The pall of downsizing hung over us nearly all the time, and no one wanted to talk about it. I remember one day Bev said she thought about the district atmosphere in relation to Maslow's law (Maslow's theoretical hierarchy of needs). Employees were not taking care of their basic needs, like rest, because they feared being next to go (Maslow's physiological need). Their security was threatened. Many had worked on the district for years, but no longer felt safe (Maslow's safety need). Their friends were leaving, people they loved, had dinner with, whose children went to school with theirs, suddenly left the office. Relationships were being destroyed (Maslow's love/belonging need). For those who remained, doing more with less compromised feelings of accomplishment (Maslow's esteem need). Lastly, downsizing kept employees from reaching their full potential.

A lot of employees felt that these trends did not affect management. Top managers seemingly did nothing to address the bleeding of jobs and lives. Downsizing affected women disproportionately because most of them held the lowest-level positions and were usually the first to go. The loss of employees all over the region left most people afraid of layoffs. I got to know the employees well, partly because of Bev, who knew their stories, and also because we socialized off-district. We even had a group that got together at the coast one weekend a month in the summertime. We called ourselves the "bad girls" and had t-shirts made. Our "bad" simply referenced the fact that when we were away from the district, we talked openly about topics that would have been frowned on, like how things really were in the office. We saw the title as a badge of honor, that we were "bad" enough to take on the issues causing tension around us. All of these women loved the district and the Forest Service, and so did I. My goal was to build morale among the women. They needed support.

There were also some men on our district who didn't feel appreciated. Ken, the wildlife biologist, was tired of butting heads with Herb, frustrated about struggling to simply do his job. This type of conflict was happening all over the nation between rangers and specialists. As the specialists made decisions based on science and ecological diversity, rangers who still operated on an old-time timber-culture model directed them, usually in the interest of maximizing timber sales, and sometimes in contradiction to environmental laws. Those tensions hit the district hard.

Leadership and Heartbreak

It seemed to me that the same hierarchy that prevented interpersonal interactions also made employees feel devalued and kept them silent. They loved the district, loved the land, but felt unappreciated and disrespected. These are things they talked with me about, issues I thought were important. I was the assistant ranger. I was management, but I had spent most of my career in subservient roles. It occurred to me that maybe I could do something to address the employees' plight. My major attempt at leadership focused on addressing this heartbreaking situation. As assistant ranger, maybe I could bring the issues that poisoned morale to the forefront. Maybe I could make things better for Herb *and* district employees, especially the women, who seemed to hurt the most.

I started by gathering information about the district's emotional climate and morale. That was not a bad start, but then I went off track by ignoring the chain of command. I did not talk with Herb. I thought the solution was bigger than my ranger, who hadn't addressed these pressures at all. Instead I took the issues of low morale, women being ignored, and Herb's moving right along like everything was fine and dandy to the acting forest supervisor, John Nelson, Mike Kerrick's replacement. This was my first mistake. Why didn't I have the wits to know that this situation was the last thing John wanted to deal with? The issue of morale meant dealing with feelings, and that was hard. Without thinking through the many problems of a forest supervisor, I went directly to John because I felt the need was immediate and monumental for workforce health. I now see that John likely had different priorities that were already embedded in his workload. Still, he listened carefully as I took what I also viewed as a benign solution to him for consideration.

I suggested we bring someone in from the outside, an objective contractor experienced in solving organizational problems, preferably a man, since a woman might have a hard time gaining credibility with the all-male management team. This person could interview folks, make a report that John, Herb, and I would discuss, and we could make a plan. This was my next mistake. I soon realized that, since many of our issues were relationship-oriented, a woman might do a better job of listening and identifying the core problems. So, I sent an email telling John that I liked an idea he had suggested, of a team approach, and that I didn't see Herb as "technically incompetent," but I noted, "It's about relationships." Herb seemed to think that grievances came from angry, vindictive women, making them less than legitimate. If we wanted to be whole again, we needed to involve everyone in building an action plan. We had to create trust. I thought intervention would move us "toward a healthy work environment for all." How wrong I was. John had agreed but told me to keep this "between us." He was uncomfortable talking about it without Herb's knowledge.

The result was that neither John nor the permanent forest supervisor who followed him did anything, possibly because of my final mistake. Soon after I had stirred the hornet's nest, I got an opportunity for a stint as acting district ranger on the Ashland Ranger District. I felt bad about leaving, but I took it. I had to follow the best path for my future, something my friends at Rigdon supported. Even so, district employees had counted on improvement. People had confided in me, hoping I would change the environment. They counted on our relationships and the fact that I cared.

By leaving, I became yet another manager getting a shot at self-actualization and leaving them in pain. I could walk away, but they no longer had an advocate. Downsizing hit the employees hard, and management did not seem to care. My exit reinforced that feeling, even though they knew personally that I cared. Soon after I left, a new forest supervisor, Darrel Kenops came to the forest. He had his own issues, and I wasn't there to push for healing. My proposal dropped away.

I later learned that Herb was angry about my interference. He should have been. He trusted me, I ruined everything, and nothing changed. Many of the women on the district said that at least I had listened and tried to effect change. No one had stepped up before. I still have friends there from that time period, so I know they didn't fault me, but I blame myself for leaving before things got better.

I Am a District Ranger

I was still officially with the Rigdon District as assistant ranger, but from January 1993 to March 1994 I worked as acting district ranger, GS-13, on the Ashland Ranger District. I should have been elated when the forest supervisor offered me a district ranger job the next year at Ashland. By then, I'd had plenty of experience to prepare me. I'd been in the forest with the biologists and learned why we needed to put logs back in streams. I'd watched preparations for timber sales and knew the meanings of the different colors painted on the trees. I'd seen the trees blown apart to create snags and understood their importance to the ecosystem. Most importantly, I had gained confidence. I knew how things worked on the ground and had a clear understanding of the hierarchy and roles—ranger on a district, professional staff, and employees.

All this, combined with my extensive early experience with the Forest Service, convinced me that it was time to enter the line. I was ready for my own district! Everyone saw this as a great opportunity for me and believed I should take the job at Ashland—everyone, that is, except me.

The offer was not to exceed (NTE) one year, and I didn't like that. The story was that women were being fast-tracked into the line, but the average time for women to become district rangers was ten to twenty years,[1] and I had been with the Forest Service since 1974. I had been an assistant district ranger for two and a half years by then. I had my twenty years of service. Basically, the NTE status of the job meant I might be assigned there permanently or I might have to work NTE at another district when the position ended.

No one had discussed the region's long-range plan for me, and I no longer had the mentorship of John Butruille and Mike Kerrick. Without this discussion, and with concern about the potential for failure, I wondered things like, *How long will it take to build a solid relationship with the staff and employees? What if something goes wrong? How will they judge me in such a short time period, with no time to address mistakes?* Everyone knows the first year is for learning about the job, and I was tired of being "the trainee." I was already a ranger, but regional management would not allow me a real leadership position. I wondered if my advocacy for women and bypassing authority as assistant ranger on the Rigdon District had played into the decision. I didn't know the answers and had no one to ask, so I decided to make a new plan, and it didn't include Forest Service.

I could take the job and show them I'm ready, I thought, *but this position puts me a year behind in my goals.* I had decided to be a GS-13 ranger within the next year. *I will not settle for less.* I had given myself three years to move up and put in the time as assistant and as acting ranger. My experience as ranger at Ashland reinforced my belief that I could and should do the job, because I *was* doing it. I managed the staff, held meetings and discussions with specialists, determined the work plan, and directed implementation. I knew the Forest Service lingo and the science of wilderness. I had the background to make important decisions and had gained the necessary experience. I had ridden the horse along a canyon, put up my tent, memorized tree names, tromped through the woods, supervised broad-scale planning, and worked at nearly every level of Forest Service. After my detail, I thought I *would* be the next ranger, not that I *might* be next. The NTE offer felt like a slap in the face. It was time for a change. But what next?

Goodbye Forest Service

The answer came when I had lunch in Portland with my friend Marilyn Johnson, whose husband worked for Forest Service. We had become friends when I worked in Portland, and we remain friends to this day. Marilyn was a personnel officer for the Bureau of Land Management (BLM), a sister organization to the Forest Service, and our lunch included BLM's Oregon State director, Elaine Zielinski. I told them about the NTE job and why I didn't want it, and that's when the solution came. Elaine was advertising a line officer job. "I would love to see you working for the BLM," she told me. That day, Elaine and Marilyn became the wind beneath my wings, and my friends for life. I've always known that you need support to achieve your goals. When it looked like my support had ended in the Forest Service, I turned to the BLM.

Even before I went to work for Elaine, I knew she would be a strong advocate because of her reputation for leadership and support for women. I remember hearing that she took the female leadership on an annual trip to the Oregon coast, an approach similar to my style on the Rigdon Ranger District. We both knew such connections built morale for the women, who desperately needed it in this man's world. I also heard that the men complained about the women going away together. Elaine responded by noting that no one complained when the men went hunting, golfing, or fishing without the women.

Elaine, a female leader whose position as director equaled that of the regional forester for Forest Service, paid attention to my career accomplishments, and to me. I got the job, and I'm pleased to say that, while working for Elaine Zielinski, I participated in the wonderful camaraderie she created to develop career success for women. I'm grateful that when I left the Forest Service, I fell under her mentorship. When I later left BLM, those same women reminded me they were only a phone call away if I needed support. I am proud to say that Elaine and most of the BLM women and I still come together when we get a call for help or friendship, even after retirement. I have not seen anyone with the kind of leadership Elaine provided for both men and women under her tutelage, except maybe Nancy Graybeal of the Forest Service, who helped me later.

Despite my never having worked for BLM, my diverse Forest Service career helped me get the job. When Forest Service leadership heard I was leaving, no one, to my knowledge, worked to help me stay. I was disappointed, hurt, and even a little angry. I had done all of this work to advance, uprooted my family to move west, and my first real line officer job came from the Bureau of Land Management, not the Forest Service. I think I had a right to be upset.

Losing my husband was the biggest emotional loss of my life, but leaving the Forest Service and Rigdon also stand among the big traumas, because it meant the end of relationships and leaving a community I had grown to love. Leaving Forest Service meant major loss. Adversity can strengthen you if you persevere, and I knew I would. Rigdon had been my first real line leadership job and leaving was hard, especially because I had not improved the environment as I'd hoped. But I had ambitions. It was time to say goodbye to my Forest Service friends. So, off I went to Eastern Oregon and the BLM.

Hello Bureau of Land Management

Working for the BLM meant moving from westside Eugene to eastside Baker City, a part of Oregon I had visited only when I drove to remote Silver Lake, where local law enforcement stopped me for driving while black. Did I have reservations about moving to Eastern Oregon, cowboy country and home on the range? I would be lying if I said I didn't. But I was more excited than afraid. I'd heard the landscape was stunning, with breathtaking views all around, and I thrive on challenges. I looked forward to many firsts and felt grateful for the awesome opportunity Elaine gave me.

I left a gray, rainy Eugene early in the morning on March 1, 1994, and arrived in Baker City to a beautiful sunny, eastside day. I had heard that Eastern Oregon got much less rain than the westside—twelve to thirteen inches versus forty-three in the Willamette Valley—and I witnessed the dry beauty right away. Once I found the perfect ranch-style house in Baker city, I returned to Eugene and supervised packing my household goods before my March 29 report date.

Working for the bureau was a natural transition for me. The government had birthed the BLM out of the General Land Office and the US Grazing Service in 1946, and the bureau had many similarities to the Forest Service. Both organizations connect to the public, with the BLM mission to "sustain the health, diversity and productivity of the public lands for the use and enjoyment of present and future generations."[2] Replace "public lands" with the "nation's forests and grasslands," in the Forest Service mission and the goals are nearly the same. Both focus on use, rather than preservation, of natural resources. Both agencies also manage a lot of land in the Northwest. Federal lands make up more than half of the State of Oregon and a quarter of Washington State.[3] BLM administers 15.7 million acres in Oregon, nearly 25 percent of the state's land base. Most is public land (13.5 million acres), but some oversight occurs on forested Oregon & California (O&C) Railroad lands.[4] BLM focused primarily on range management but, like Forest Service, had to contend with the spotted owl controversy that transformed the "get out the cut" management of timber stands. In fact, like Forest Service, BLM reduced harvests dramatically, with the 1.5 billion board feet harvested in 1986 from its O&C lands decreased to 160 million board feet by 2010.

TABLE 1

US Department of the Interior Mission Statement	US Department of Agriculture Mission and Vision
The Department of the Interior protects and manages the Nation's natural resources and cultural heritage; provides scientific and other information about those resources; and honors its trust responsibilities or special commitments to American Indians, Alaska Natives, and affiliated island communities. (US Department of the Interior website, https://www.doi.gov/whoweare/Mission-Statement)	We provide leadership on food, agriculture, natural resources, rural development, nutrition, and related issues based on public policy, the best available science, and effective management. We have a vision to provide economic opportunity through innovation, helping rural America to thrive; to promote agriculture production that better nourishes Americans while also helping feed others throughout the world; and to preserve our Nation's natural resources through conservation, restored forests, improved watersheds, and healthy private working lands. Our strategic goals serve as a roadmap for the Department to help ensure we achieve our mission and implement our vision. (US Department of Agriculture website, https://www.usda.gov/our-agency/about-usda)

There were some differences between the agencies (see table 1). The Department of the Interior manages BLM, while the Department of Agriculture operates Forest Service. That difference became important to me because the Interior Department's focus on cultural heritage meant my new job as Baker Resource Area manager included natural *and cultural* resources oversight.

The Vale District in Ontario, Oregon, the regional BLM office, was comparable to a forest supervisor's office. It provided administration for the Malheur and Jordan Resource Areas, with the Baker Resource Area "detached" and located about ninety miles away from Vale, where I attended monthly team meetings. My Baker Resource Area included the Snake River and Hells Canyon Complex, with the breathtaking Steens Mountain in the Jordan Resource Area.

The ten-mile-long Hells Canyon is stupendous. Rocky buttes jut upward on both sides of the Snake River, the longest north–south waterway on the continent and the deepest gorge in North America. A writer named William Ashworth described Hells Canyon perfectly:

> Awesome, . . . incredibly deep, austerely magnificent, it slashes between the states of Oregon and Idaho like a raw and gaping wound. To stand on the rim and gaze into that vast hole is to know humility as few places can teach it; to venture into it is to enter a place apart, a separate world-within-a-world where the old scales and comfortable concepts of size and distance fade into irrelevancy.[5]

The magnificent neighboring Steens that rises to nearly ten thousand feet is also like a basalt island, its jagged peaks interspersed with layers of green in springtime, so beautiful that I immediately and regularly connected with the Jordan resource manager, Bruce Johnson. Bruce always called to tell me when he had a show-me trip to the Steens, and I always accepted, time permitting.

The position of resource area manager in the BLM is comparable to district ranger in the Forest Service. Both are responsible for employees, programs, and the land under their jurisdiction. The difference is in organizational focus. In the West, Forest Service focuses primarily on timber management, fire, and recreation. BLM emphasizes range management, but includes some timber and recreation. Oil and gas was another big program, but not on my resource area, though I did deal with mining. One of the major differences between the entities is geographical. National forests are contiguous, with few inholdings, whereas BLM has a checkerboard land base. This scattered pattern occurred because, in the 1860s, the federal government transferred more than forty million acres of land out of the public domain for railroad and wagon road land grants. Railroad companies, including the Oregon & California Railroad, received odd-numbered sections of land they were required to sell to "actual settlers" to finance construction and boost the economy. When O&C violated the grant terms, Congress reclaimed 2.5 million acres as federal lands. In 1937, Congress directed management of those lands for timber production. This resulted in a disconnected land configuration with multiple sections owned by ranchers, interspersed with public domain managed by BLM. This history made management complicated, since government conservation efforts had to happen in concert with private land owners.[6]

Luckily, I had help in my dealings with the ranchers and others. After settling in, I regularly went straight to the house of my special friend Kathy Corn after work to talk. Kathy would listen attentively while we ate and drank evening libations. She said I needed to know the players in Baker City. Both realtors with a brokerage firm, Kathy and her husband Jerry knew just about everyone in town. We had a plan. Before I met someone new, I would get feedback from the staff and then call Kathy to confirm, invalidate, or add information. I did this until I knew the stakeholders myself. Kathy helped in other ways, too. She even gave my son a job when he joined me in Baker City to attend Eastern Oregon University.

Baker City Resource Area on the Oregon Trail

My first day in the office I met my two assistants, Dorothy Mason and Larry Anderson, and my third assistant, and manager of the National Historic Oregon Trail Interpretive Center (NHOTIC), Dave Hunsaker. All three were longtime Baker Resource Area (BRA) employees and very knowledgeable about resources, projects, and history, something I valued highly. In fact, all the employees lived in Baker City as well as the BRA.

This included May Ohman, the archeologist, and Dick Hanson, who was both a mining specialist and in charge of timber.

Dorothy and Larry used the first day to introduce me to the employees and go over current projects and the environmental assessments that supported them. They had a map of the entire resource area with colored dots showing project locations and trouble spots, like where cows stayed too close to the river or overgrazed. To my surprise, the map showed that the area boundary went into extreme Eastern Oregon and southeastern Washington, which made for long overnight field trips. These briefings took all day, so I was surprised, tired, and delighted when they took me to an all-employees room, with food everywhere and an opportunity to talk one-on-one with employees. As always, bonding over a meal got things started on the right track.

The next day it was David's turn to brief me on the NHOTIC, the cultural resources piece of my job and a national jewel. I joined Dave for the briefing at the interpretive center, where I could meet and greet employees and see the displays. David spoke almost poetically about NHOTIC, his voice and body language revealing how much he loved it—his baby. Dave reminded me of a colonel in the army because he wore period clothes, uniform, and hat nearly all the time. The center had come into being when Oregon's governor sought economic development plans to combat unemployment rates of 18 to 22 percent, and Baker City proposed focusing on cultural tourism. Not only had the idea for NHOTIC come from the community, but David, who helped to develop it, recently told me that "without BLM'S local and state leadership and the community, the center would not have happened." I arrived just two years after the center's grand opening on May 23, 1992, when ten thousand people visited in a three-day period. "There were other BLM centers," says Dave, "but NHOTIC had the most detailed exhibits at the time, right down to the dirt under the fingernails."[7]

I have visited many interpretive centers, but I could not believe what I saw here, and I immediately understood Dave's passion; NHOTIC was stunning. Baker City sits in a valley with the Mission Mountains on one side and the Wallowas on the other. The center stands on a hill at the end of the Oregon Trail above the town. From afar, the buildings that make up the center appear like three huge covered wagons set in a half circle, with a minute opening between each. Ribbed canvas stretches overhead so that, from inside, the domed ceiling still looks like the curve of a covered wagon.

I remember thinking, *God this looks so real!* The production spared no attention to detail. The simulated terrain looked rugged and weathered, with hoof marks suggesting animal passage. They even figured out how to make ruts in the trail! David told me that each sagebrush plant and blade of grass had been chemically treated and then colored by hand to match living vegetation. A contracted muralist created the land- and sky-scape backdrop using techniques perfected by da Vinci and Michelangelo in the Middle Ages. The best part may have been the mannequins. Lines of oxen pull wagons, while mothers and children walk on one side, with Native people on opposite hillsides. As young men lead the oxen or herd sheep ahead, others make camp nearby. In one scene, a young girl kneels next to a wooden cross on the rocky ground spattered with Oregon sagebrush. So lifelike were these figures that facial expressions reveal everything from a mother's exhaustion to a child's joy, with details like beard stubble and veins in a mannequin's hands simulating reality. I was proud to supervise management of this exquisite center, a collaborative venture financed through community and government funding to make Baker City a tour-ist destination.

Special events added another dimension to the visitor experience. My second year, we celebrated the center's anniversary with the community, employees, and me dressed up in period clothes as pioneers. We had a gold mine staging area for visitors to learn the process, or they could sit inside a covered wagon and taste food made from Oregon Trail recipes. A local rancher loaned us his oxen to tie up behind the wagon. My son and his girlfriend, Nichole, demonstrated a wedding by jumping the broom, a ritual used by slaves when they married. (Later, Andre and Nichole did marry, but in a church!) We finished up with a one-person play by Joyce Hunsaker playing Sacagawea (then Sacajawea), a Shoshone woman who accompanied Lewis and Clark on their journey to the Pacific in 1805. What a fun day—so much talent. When I think of Baker City, I realize that part of my joy in that job came from this kind of interaction with visitors, the community, and center employees.

Native Lands and Reconciliation

A lot of exciting activities in my new job related to cultural issues. Although the Oregon Trail Center exhibits included Native people, they did not deal with the very real history related to colonization, treaty-making, and relocating Indians to reservations in the 1850s—to make way for pioneers. The BLM focused instead on positive interactions between Native people and new arrivals. Indian mannequins appeared to watch pioneers from afar or trade with them at a campfire. Such depictions of the connections between settlers and Indian people left out the very important land loss that resulted from Oregon's resettlement by pioneer immigrants. For example, the traditional Nez Perce land base had been reduced from more than seven million acres to approximately 700,000 acres under the 1863 "steal treaty," which took away lands in the Wallowa Mountains, where the tribe had lived for millennia. Forced relocation to a reservation at Lapwai, Idaho, followed in 1877, under General Oliver Otis Howard.[8]

General Howard had fought on the Union side of the Civil War as a believer in the end of slavery. Afterward, Howard administered the Freedmen's Bureau, the Reconstruction Era agency that supported newly freed people and refugees by issuing rations, clothing and medicine; helping people find their families; and building schools and providing teachers. The major task of the bureau was to settle formerly enslaved people onto land, to provide tools, seed, and draft animals, and to arrange work contracts with white landowners. As part of his continuing work, the general helped found Howard University, a school of high academic standing in Washington, DC, where I grew up, specifically for educating newly freed slaves. So, I knew who he was.

Ironically, Howard, who came to Vancouver Barracks in 1874, then became part of a great wrong done by the government to the Indian people by leading the chase in the Nez Perce War, as several bands of "non-treaty" Nez Perce sought freedom across the border in Canada. From June to October 1877, the army hunted down bands of Nez Perce who refused an ultimatum to go to the reservation. Ultimately, many Indian people were killed in skirmishes, while others almost starved. The army captured the remainder and sent about four hundred Nez Perce far away to "Indian Country" in Oklahoma. Several children died along the way, and nearly two of three who made the trip became ill, many with malaria. Without enough medicine, forty-seven Nez Perce died in their first two months away from the Northwest. When Joseph and his band returned to the West in 1885, only 268 remained alive. Of the survivors, 118 went to the Nez Perce Reservation at Lapwai, Idaho. The army sent the remainder, along with Joseph, to the Colville Reservation in Washington Territory. Still, Joseph and other non-treaty Nez Perce never gave up the idea of getting back their traditional lands near the Wallowas, where their ancestors lay. After the chief's death in 1904, the tribe continuously tried to follow through with his dreams.[9]

That's where I came in. I learned this story when tribal representatives came to ask whether I could help them retrieve ten thousand acres of highly valued traditional land currently owned by a local rancher. My office had done several land exchanges seeking to geographically reconnect our checkerboard holdings, and it occurred to me that we might use the same process to facilitate an exchange between the tribe and the landowner. Since priority projects occupied my staff, I was honored to take this task on myself.

I started by meeting repeatedly with the landowner, showing him places on the map I thought might interest him for exchange, but he always responded sullenly. I could tell he did not like me or my proposals. I remember him saying, "Why would you think I want to participate in this?" and "How would that BLM land be worth my land?" But I kept trying and even brought my staff together to see if they had any ideas. That's when I learned the backstory. My range conservation land officer explained that we had rescinded the rancher's allotment, because he had left his cows to overwinter there, despite the rules. One of our cow-counting surveys showed overgrazing and several dead cows in the aftermath. There was no way in hell the rancher would work with me. I was devastated. The pride I had in taking on this project left me crying over my defeat. I was one minority trying to right an injustice suffered by another. The failure weighed heavily on me, and I dreaded returning to the tribe, knowing these deserving people would be disappointed once again.

But, I'm no quitter! I remembered some work I had done earlier with the Trust for Public Lands, a nonprofit organization that facilitates and funds the creation of parks and protected lands. I called them and asked for help. They agreed to take over the process, and I left the picture. I was

ecstatic to later learn that the trust successfully returned the land to the
tribe a year after I left Baker City. The trust and the Nez Perce invited my
staff and the new area manager to the ceremony. I couldn't go, but was
there in spirit.

We think of reconciliation as a way to fix injustices of the past, but it
never successfully erases the pain from one generation to the next. Minority people who have been persecuted will always remember the anguish
and pass stories of trauma down to their children. I had seen this in my
own community and in the history of the Nez Perce people. I was glad to
play a small part in righting a tiny segment of the wrongs done to them.

Work on the Ground

Working with Native people stands out as among the best parts of my
job, but managing a resource area of this size had a lot of different com-
ponents. Three other major areas stand out in my memory: working with
ranchers, weed control, and the bureaucratic responsibilities of managing
lands that include stakeholders of all types, public and private, state and
federal. I was area manager for Baker in the mid-1990s, as environmental
backlash cropped up all over the country. Like the Forest Service, the
BLM continuously dealt with shifting practices affected by law. In those
days, we did a lot of things under the radar, because the public, industry,
and environmentalists watched closely and reacted to everything done
by our neighbors, the Forest Service, in the Wallowa-Whitman National
Forest. For example, we used herbicides that the Forest Service, then
under injunction, could not. But we did so quietly.

An important part of our charge was weed control in use areas, like
recreation sites and where livestock concentrate. Control was critical
because noxious invasive plants like Scotch thistle, with its tiny dande-
lion-like seeds that can blow for miles, have a competitive advantage over
native plants. Not only can Scotch thistle alter delicate ecosystems by
spreading rapidly, it grows in patches of spiny plants that can block recreational access and harm animals. Smart cows stay away from it, but many
try to eat it and get poked around the mouth and eyes, resulting in fester-
ing sores. Even if cattle don't consume Scotch thistle, the plant's presence
reduces other food sources. Dead plants also contribute to fire danger.
This was one reason we used herbicides, even though we suspected they

were not environmentally safe for water systems, animals, or people. Sometimes the job of a manager crosses personal boundaries. This was one of those times for me. I disliked using potentially harmful chemicals, but my staff had to get rid of the weeds. Professionally I had a job to do, even if it did not always sit right with me.

The checkerboard ownership program in the Baker Resource Area also caused problems, such as ranchers who let cows trespass on federal lands without permits. I decided to face this problem directly by meeting with ranchers around their kitchen tables to discuss keeping their cows out of creeks. Fecal matter from too many cows in the water can cause algae blooms, kill fish, and pollute water sources used by humans. This meant we and the ranchers needed to work together to prevent contamination. I felt that making personal contact at home established far better rapport and trust than having ranchers come to my office. I must have been right, because I developed friendly relationships with many of them.

I remember one night while having a beer after work, a rancher named Richard Ames told me about his pregnant cow. I had never seen a calf born, so he offered to call me and send a car to pick me up when she went into labor. I agreed, not thinking about how baby calves could be born at different times of day, just like our human babies. I was not happy to get a 3:00 a.m. wake-up call one night, but still I went. Not only was it the middle of the night, but the calf was a breech birth. Seven grueling hours later, it came. I made a mental note that I would never watch a calf birth again. I recall thinking that birthing human babies leaves you with wonderful feelings—calves, not so much. I was nauseous and late for work. Looking back, I think I may have judged my first calving experience too harshly. Witnessing birth in a barn, in the wild, or at a hospital, is miraculous no matter what.

One of the more complex issues I dealt with also brought together several different stakeholders. The area was dealing with the Federal Energy Regulation Commission (FERC) relicensing for the three dams built by Idaho Power Company on the Snake River, which runs along BLM and Forest Service lands and separates Oregon and Idaho. Brownlee Dam, the largest of the privately owned Hells Canyon Complex, had been completed in 1959 and backed up fifty-seven miles of reservoir, creating some of the most highly fished waters in Idaho. Next came Oxbow (1961) and Hells Canyon (1967) Dams, also part of the complex. None of these dams included fish passage for the anadromous salmon that migrated each year to the Upper Snake River Basin. All included hydroelectric power production that profited Idaho Power. For that reason, the company built recreation sites, boat ramps, and fishing areas as part of the trade-off for dam construction, making the Snake River a destination spot.

The current license was due to expire in 2005, and it was our job to provide information to FERC for that relicensing. FERC is an independent agency that regulates the interstate transmission of electricity, natural gas, and oil. The agency also reviews proposals to build liquefied natural gas terminals and interstate natural gas pipelines, as well as licensing hydropower projects, including those on BLM land. We, along with the Forest Service, had to provide input so the power company met the needs of the land and communities as it headed toward relicensing. Over the years, the number of users had increased significantly, so relicensing conditions should include paying for additional sites and upgrades to the existing infrastructure.

This work took a lot of time, driving back and forth to Idaho Power Company headquarters in Boise, a place that seemed like the big city compared to Baker City. We would haul reams of paper and maps to meetings with the company lawyers, men who looked like New Yorkers in their expensive suits and Gucci shoes. I wore jeans and cowboy boots to see the ranchers, but I put on Misook and Burberry for those meetings. Negotiations were ongoing for the entire time I was there, and when I left in 1997, talks continued. Dorothy Mason, my former assistant who is now retired from BLM, says the documentation is finished and still awaits FERC's relicensing decision. Since 2005, Idaho Power has done business without a license, all the while making a lot of money.

Leaving the Pacific Northwest

Other highlights from working in the area included a visit by Mike Dombeck, the director of BLM (later chief forester) and Elaine Zielinski, state director for Oregon and Washington, who presented us with a regional award for our weed program. Award day was bittersweet because of my internal conflict. I had not wanted to use chemicals, but my job required me to get rid of the noxious weeds. That was my rationale. I felt accomplished, but my conscience nagged me. To this day, the BLM uses herbicides and pesticides to manage invasive species, and they do it under very specific guidelines.[10]

On a lighter note, I was thrilled about my other two awards. The Cattlemen's Association and the Miners' Association each made me an honorary member. These honors tied directly to the work my staff and I did with ranchers and miners during my tenure. Ranchers appreciated my attendance at their meetings, and that I worked with them individually. The miners were pleased that my staff had been assigned to help them interpret new regulations and complete paperwork requiring them to accurately document the locations of their claims, alongside annual assessments of their activities. I was proud of those endorsements, especially because of the notoriously conflictual relationships among federal agencies, ranchers, and miners.

This had been my best assignment to date. But about three years into my stint as area manager, my mom had a heart attack. She needed surgery to place two stents in her heart, so I flew back to Washington, DC. The stents helped, but my mom remained in precarious health. It didn't take me long to decide: instead of returning to Oregon, I would live at home and help take care of my mother. I asked for a transfer, and Elaine helped me find a BLM job in the Division of Resources Planning, Use and Protection for Eastern States. I could stay in DC. I knew I would miss the smell of the mountain air after rain, our abundant and glorious spring flowers, the majestic mountains on the eastside and westside, the hundreds of miles to walk and ride bicycles, the Pacific Ocean, and the massive number of stars. I hated leaving the beauty of the Northwest, but my family needed me.

CHAPTER 6

Rebirth on Mount St. Helens

WITH MY MOTHER ILL AND A NEW BLM JOB as branch chief of adjudication, my stress level was high. I supervised the Eastern States Lands and Realty Program, a position comparable to Forest Service assistant director in the WO. This job took me into the administrative arena, but without forest or mountains to soothe my soul and compensate for the detailed paperwork. The bureau administered all transactions on public lands that were not under another federal agency. The adjudication department authorized purchases and acquisitions, sales and exchanges, withdrawals and rights of way. That means we defined boundaries, maintained public land records, and produced environmental assessments for commercial filming and recreation activities. For me, the job at the eastern states program provided another opportunity to learn about and participate in the work of government at a higher level. From that perspective, it was valuable experience, but it was *so* boring!

A critical responsibility included managing the bureau's automated land status data system, which contained information on surveyed lands as far back as the 1800s and was available to the public by appointment. We also ran the oil and gas leasing program and dealt with industry scouts seeking oil speculation opportunities. Once they identified desired parcels, industry representatives submitted "expressions of interest" for specific sites. My staff then reviewed them for compliance with our resource management plan and to identify any conflicts that made the parcels ineligible. My staff and I also traveled quarterly to different locations to conduct public competitive bidding sales for these parcels.

The travel was fun but did not offset the worst part of this job, an issue that went beyond boring paperwork—managing incompetent personnel. Of the sixty employees who worked for me, it seemed a third took no pride in their jobs. They were lazy and engaged in varying degrees of misconduct, from missing deadlines to ignoring procedures. Some employees came in late without explanation or spent hours at lunch and then claimed full days on their timesheets. That really irked me, and as the supervisor I felt obligated to hold them accountable. I soon learned that a lot of employees (and management) knew about the issues in my department, but no one had done anything about it.

In defense of management, the immediate supervisor is responsible for holding employees accountable. That meant me. As department manager, I tried to improve efficiency by putting each of these employees on a PIPR (personnel improvement performance review). A PIPR is a tool used to document and address the behavior and actions of problem employees. Putting together a PIPR is time-consuming if you are doing it for one employee. I did it for several once I had decided, so it took me six weeks to collect the information I needed for my supervisor. I did this mostly during late nights at the office. So, imagine my surprise when my supervisor asked me to find another way to deal with the situation. I said "Another way? We have grounds to suspend them." But, like Rigdon, management proved reluctant to deal with tough employee issues.

I later learned that these same employees—all black women—had brought and won discrimination suits against BLM, which resulted in promotions to the very jobs for which I wanted them held accountable. Letting this behavior slide insulted the dedicated employees who did their jobs well. This abuse of the system by some people of color is the very reason that policies like affirmative action got a bad name in the first place. I had worked too hard to let this group represent me or to tolerate it in my own department!

I had spent a decade taking jobs that enabled me to work with trustworthy and reliable employees in serene, beautiful surroundings that inspired me to be better—as an employee and a human being. Now, I found myself in an environment where people simply accepted poor work ethics, which embarrassed me and other black people. I began to think I did not belong there. I needed to decide if I could continue doing the job. Thank God my mom was getting better, because I didn't know how much longer I could take the work situation. When one of the problem employees keyed my car in the parking lot while I worked at my desk, I decided I was done. I knew who did it, and I wanted to take her to an alley and kick her ass. This is what I would have done when I was sixteen years old, but I'd left that Gloria behind long ago. Now I had to be the adult in the room. Now, I had to preserve my own sanity. This required leaving my job—and my mom.

I humbled myself and called Nancy Graybeal, deputy regional forester in Portland, and asked if there was a job that I could apply for. I knew that Nancy did her best to support the men and women under her, and I hoped I was still one of those people. I wanted to return to the Forest Service and to the Northwest. Not only had I hated my job at the Eastern States Land and Realty Program, the hustle and bustle, constant traffic, and massive numbers of people in DC had assaulted my senses. Thanks to Nancy I was able to go home to the Northwest. I asked Mom to come, too, but she said, "Gloria my own mom, sisters and brother live here. Your father is buried here. I understand you need to leave. I left Georgia and my mom over forty years ago. Now this is my home." I told her I loved her and I understood. I left determined never to accept another job in Washington, DC.

I'm a Westerner Now

I headed back to Region 6 in December 1997 with a heavy heart. Moving across country this time wasn't any easier than it had been before, even though my mom said she understood, but returning to the Northwest relieved my sorrow. Back east I was surrounded with concrete buildings, crowds of people, and too many cars. I had missed the beautiful green forests; the diverse landscapes, mountains, and waterfalls; mild breezes and soft rain; and the hordes of stars when I looked up in the sky. I may not have been born there, but I now considered myself a certified westerner. I knew then that I would never live anywhere else. I was taking a coveted position in the Forest Service, monument manager for Mount St. Helens (MSH) National Volcanic Monument on the Gifford Pinchot National Forest in Washington State. I have no doubt that my successful tenure managing the National Historic Oregon Trail Interpretive Center in Baker City helped me land the job.

I remembered the scene that ultimately made my new job possible. Mount St. Helens had erupted on May 18, 1980, several years before I headed west the first time. I had watched with the rest of the world as the mountain blew its top, sparked by an earthquake that registered 5.1 on the Richter scale. Both the summit and its north slope collapsed, as "gas rich magma and super-heated groundwater" blasted out of the mountain's side and mixed with rock and debris to "create concrete-like mudflows that scoured [surrounding] river valleys." It took less than three minutes for 230 square miles of forestland to disappear, flattened by the largest landslide ever recorded. Next, a huge plume of volcanic ash and pumice blasted up to fifteen miles high and turned day to night across much of the Northwest, completely darkening the sky in Spokane, Washington, 250 miles away. "Avalanches of super-heated gas and pumice, called pyroclastic flows, swept down the flanks of the volcano," continuing, along with mudflows, through the day and into the next night. The blast killed more than fifty people, created a "gray wasteland," wiped out wildlife and plants, and economically destroyed nearby communities.[1] Within three days, the ash cloud spread across the country, and within fifteen days it circled the earth. For weeks after that, glassy slivers of gray ash covered houses and cars from eastern Washington to Portland, while major ash falls blew into the sky as far as central Montana. It even reached the Great Plains.[2]

As I had watched the television in shock, I realized I was witnessing another disaster of major proportions. I had seen people attacked by dogs and water hoses on TV during the civil rights movement of the 1960s. The TV brought me right to the assassinations of John F. Kennedy, Robert F. Kennedy, and Dr. Martin Luther King Jr., and I had seen the riots in Washington, DC, and across the country, along with protests against the Vietnam War. I recall thinking of the eruption on MSH as another disaster that would affect many lives, but it never occurred to me that I would one day know the mountain intimately.

In the wake of the eruption, Congress had passed the Mount St. Helens National Volcanic Monument Act of 1982, signed by President Ronald Reagan. The act created a national monument, with a land base that included the crater itself and 110,000 acres of land sprouting with renewed life after almost total destruction. The act also provided special funding for education, interpretation, and scientific monitoring, all managed by the US Forest Service. Our agency and Congress had a grand vision, and it was no wonder. The earth itself had unexpectedly created an opportunity for humans to witness the rebirth of an ecosystem. This emergent life could also fuel economic recovery for local communities.

As the twentieth anniversary of the blast loomed, I took over the helm of the Mount St. Helens District to oversee the continuing regeneration and study of Mount St. Helens. I had more than sixty permanent employees and a budget of $4.7 million for the three interpretive centers on the mountain's east side.[3] There were approximately forty employees on the westside, where the resource projects happened. The seasonal workforce sometimes took personnel numbers as high as two hundred.

The design of the three visitor centers reflected their varied purposes. The Silver Lake Mount St. Helens Visitor Center (VC), built in 1986, provides "a gateway" to MSH, more than thirty miles away, and presents a view of the mountain's west side. Visitors typically stopped there first to see the interactive interpretive stations focused on the historical landscape and impacts to the ecosystem. Silver Lake VC is smaller than the Oregon Trail Interpretive Center, but it also includes mannequins, a large step-in model of the volcano, a functioning seismograph of the mountain, and interpretive staff.[4] By 1997, more than ten thousand people had visited Silver Lake since the opening, and in 2000 USFS leased the visitor center to Washington State Parks, consolidating its resources closer to the mountain. Forest Service finally transferred Silver Lake VC into the park system in 2007. I am sure this was due to continuing budget cuts.[5]

The next visitor center, Coldwater Ridge, stood forty-three miles east of Castle Rock on the Spirit Lake Highway and ten miles west of Johnston Ridge. Designed as a science and learning center, Coldwater's exhibits highlighted the geologic history of the volcano and included eyewitness accounts of the explosion, displays that focused on the science of monitoring volcanic activity. Visitors could also access trails with views of the lava dome, the crater, the pumice plain, and landslide deposits. By 2013, the Mount St. Helens Institute, a nonprofit that no longer involved the Forest Service, operated Coldwater Ridge as an educational and conference center. Many of the exhibits have since been removed, a change I'm sure also stemmed from budget cuts.

The last center, Johnston Ridge, is located at the campsite where David Johnston, a volcanologist with the US Geological Survey, worked and died, his trailer on the mountainside swept away just after transmitting news of the eruption. On my first visit to Johnston Ridge, I realized the eruption of MSH could not compare to anything I had ever seen before. The movie showed at the VC captured the lateral blast visually and included the mountain's roar, a sound akin to an atom bomb. I wish that every child in America could see this, without experiencing it like those who died that horrific day.

The southwest side of MSH included 450,000 acres of forested land not included in the monument designation. There we carried out our resource goals and objectives, such as timber harvest, recreational activities, wildlife conservation, and other aspects of ecosystem management. Eventually, I lived on that side of the mountain, in Amboy, a tiny town of just over two thousand people. When not managing the interpretive centers, I spent time reading EAs for timber harvest, recreation sites, and trail building and maintenance. It was a fast-paced, educational, and gratifying life that kept me busy all the time!

Home at Last

When I returned to Portland in the winter of 1997, I moved in with my boyfriend, Phil Wikelund. I had been introduced to Phil and his wife, Karen, by Vito, a man I dated when I first lived in Portland. After Karen died of cancer in 1994, Phil and I met again. I would go into his bookstore and chat with him for hours. When I moved to Eastern Oregon and he came through on business, he always stayed with me, but only as a friend. I respected Phil greatly and appreciated that he seemed to know more than I ever would in my lifetime. This is because he is an avid reader; even now, for every book I read, he's reading three or four. I also found it incredible how he could connect people who didn't know each other. This ability helped him in his career. Phil had graduated from Reed College and eventually became the sole owner of Great Northwest Bookstore. He's always wanted and needed to be his own boss, and owning the bookstore gave him the best of all worlds: reading, learning, talking, and self-management. He has never lost his love for research, knowledge, and books. It stayed strong even after Great Northwest burned down in 2010 and forced him into retirement.

Despite my admiration, I'd had no idea that Phil's Baker City visits would turn into anything more than an interesting friendship. That changed right before I left Oregon. By then, he knew I was leaving for Washington, DC, and this time when he visited, much to my surprise, he brought me flowers and wine. I realized I had been suppressing my affection, and my feelings exploded. Our romance began. The first kiss sealed it, and fondness quickly turned to passion. I didn't think it would turn into anything more, but Phil visited me several times after I moved east, and I discovered that my esteem for him went beyond his intellect. I had also valued the way he took care of Karen and made it possible for her to die at home. I kept thinking about this when we started dating. My husband had loved me like Phil loved Karen. Neither one of us thought we could ever love that way again. So far, we have now been together longer than either of us were married. This is interesting considering Phil is white, and when you think about the fact that neither of us had ever dated outside our race.

When I left DC, Phil flew there to drive with me back to Portland. We took the southern route because it was winter, and as we drove cross-country we visited his friends and his mother, Dorothy Wikelund, in Bloomington, Indiana. She had also attended Reed College and was an academic. She seemed interested in me, and was gracious, if not embracing. We also stopped in Little Rock, Arkansas, to see my daughter Catrina, who now worked for the Forest Service. Mary Albertson, who became the Forest Service Region 6 civil rights director in Portland, successfully recruited Catrina at a Portland State University job fair. Then working on a master's in public administration, Catrina called to excitedly tell me about her new position at Timber Lake Job Corps Center on the Mount Hood National Forest. She said, "Mommy, I'm going to be a counselor for the Forest Service."

I said, "Sweetheart, I'm so proud of you! You never said that you wanted to work for the Forest Service."

"I always said when I grow up, I want to be just like you. I thought that taking this job would be a good start!" I didn't know what to say after that, except that "the fruit don't fall far from the tree." I took all my children out to celebrate when we learned about Trina's new career. It was an exciting night, because everyone was doing well. Andre worked in Salem, Oregon, for Kids at Risk, a program that allowed judges to identify kids with behavior problems and match them with counselors like Andre. It was the perfect job for him because of his good humor and kindness. My oldest daughter, Nicki, had joined me in DC and now worked a management job with Marshalls department stores. When I left, she stayed in the nice house I'd purchased in Alexandria, Virginia. I was very proud of all three of my children and still am!

Catrina had been transferred to the Wichita Job Corps Center in Little Rock, Arkansas, in 1996, which is where Phil and I visited. When we arrived, she wasn't home, so we went to dinner. Phil found a strip mall in the African American part of town with a restaurant that served barbecue. I was apprehensive about being an interracial couple in Arkansas. Even in the late 1990s, interracial couples in the South were rare, and the discomfort went both ways—in the black and white communities. I worried about being heckled, or worse. I didn't want to go in, but fearless Phil insisted, and he was right. Yes, a few people stared, but we also had a great meal. No one was disrespectful, and we even received some smiles. We also had a good visit with my daughter. We spent the evening listening to her talk excitedly about working in Arkansas. She shared stories about her Job Corps students and ended with talking about her church and her pastor. The next day, after a hearty breakfast of pancakes, bacon, and scrambled eggs, we continued our trip to Portland.

When we arrived, I realized how happy I was to be back in the Pacific Northwest. Andre and Nichole were engaged to be married, and we celebrated their wedding in Portland in 1999. Soon after, they bought a new house in Salem, where Nichole worked for the state prison system, executing their education and contracts program. Despite this good news, and management status on my new job, I still felt like a widow who never had enough. I could never forget how hard life had been after my husband died. There had been the financial burdens that came with my low-wage job as a single parent with three kids before I moved west. Things improved over time as I moved up the career ladder, but then came Ronald Reagan's cuts to Social Security and the kids' increasing financial needs as teenagers. When it came to college, Andre had taken out loans and was still paying them back. Trina had a full scholarship, and Nicki already worked full time. It seemed I'd had a momentary reprieve with the job in Baker City and then my mother had become ill. Now, I hoped for some calm.

On the Road to Mount St. Helens

The ongoing financial struggle contributed to moving in with Phil when I returned to Portland. An affordable house was out of reach, and thanks to him I didn't have to worry financially. Boy, did I have a hell of a commute, though! It took me more than an hour each way to drive to Amboy from his house in Washington County and to return home—in good traffic.

I spent the first two months meeting with staff, elected officials, partners, and volunteers. I also had introductory meetings with the National Park Service (NPS) and the US Geological Survey (USGS). Both agencies had an interest in MSH, but USGS worked with us directly on our science program. Many of our research stations employed scientists, but the monument was the only regular district unit in Forest Service with a scientist on staff, Peter Frenzen, who worked closely with USGS to monitor the mountain's activity. Such scientific discovery at Mount St. Helens made the site special. Research stations investigated the blast zone and monitored everything from natural wildlife and vegetation recovery to the use of genetically engineered seedlings.

The visitor center located in Cowlitz County, Washington, added to my long-distance travel. I would go into the field to examine projects and come back to the office to return phone calls, read environmental assessments (EAs), and complete paperwork. Despite the intensity, I was as high as a kite because I loved my work. I felt honored to have such a great job, and saw it as a true stepping stone toward my future goals. But, I had so much to do and learn—I found myself staying late every night for months.

Once a month I had a light commute because I spent the day with our forest leadership team in Vancouver, Washington. The management team included Forest Supervisor Ted Stubblefield, Deputy Forest Supervisor Claire Lavendel, natural resource management staff, and district rangers from Mount Adams and the Cowlitz Valley, along with me for Mount St. Helens. Traveling to Vancouver from Washington County took only thirty-five minutes, but traveling to and from Amboy took a toll. It meant I had to leave home early, return late, and still had limited time at the office. Traffic often backed up on the I-5 bridge, which could be stressful, but even worse were the hazardous conditions on the road up to the mountains in the wintertime. Phil and I talked about it and agreed it would be safer, and in my best interests professionally, to move nearer to work.

So, I packed up my furniture, and Bibs my poodle, and moved myself to another new home, a ranger house on the district in Amboy. The move was a good idea: not only did it buy me more time and less stress, I could also focus more on district priorities. The travel time had interfered with how much I could accomplish. One priority was to change my interpretive specialists' job description from the Forest Service 1001 to the National Park Service's 024 series. The 1001 series is described as general arts and information, but the 024 series better described what the specialists did—interpretation and education. I had to work with the National Park Service (NPS) to put my argument together. Like the BLM, the NPS is in the Department of the Interior, an agency more responsible for interpretation and preservation than my own Forest Service, which focused on resource use. The local NPS superintendent agreed that their 024 series better described my interpreters' work, since all the programs in the interpretive centers were educational.

Like the Park Service, our programs served a national and international audience, and Mount St. Helens National Monument had a legal designation from Congress more like that of a national park than a national forest. Presidents could declare national monuments under the 1906 Antiquities Act, which focused on historic and archaeological sites, but also included objects of "scientific interest." That scientific interest component is what made MSH eligible for monument status. But this status made management complicated, because it meant both preservation and multiple-use management at the same time.[6]

Convincing the Forest Service to change the classification for my employees was like pulling teeth. They maintained the appropriateness of the 1001 series, but I insisted that my interpreters were not information specialists—that's what I had been in the Washington office when I answered phones. They were interpretive specialists, who helped the public understand what had happened on Mount St. Helens during the blast and now with the land's recovery. To convince human resources, I provided examples of our programs, letters of support from local Park Service officials, my supervisor, and many supporters and volunteers. Finally, ours became the only Forest Service unit to use the Park Services'

024 series. The pay was the same, but I thought it important that my employees' job descriptions matched the work they actually did.

Troubles on the Mountain

The diverse issues at Mount St. Helens often required compromise. For example, in the winter of 1999, a Suquamish tribal member killed his second elk in a week within the closure area of the monument. That was a problem for us. I knew that tribes had traditionally hunted and gathered on the national forests, but the monument status changed things. We now declared some areas off-limits to hunting and gathering for everyone, including tribes. In this case, the Suquamish man had been arrested and charged. He would either be reported to tribal officials for action or face federal charges. This created a sensitive situation between Forest Service and the tribes, and it got the attention of the media. At the heart of the matter was a clash between federal oversight and treaty rights, which had been upheld only informally on national forest land until then. We held a lot of meetings with tribal leaders, local communities, and the US Fish and Wildlife Service to figure out how to handle this situation. Since I managed the area, I had a major role in the decision making. We had to do something. Finally, we decided not to prosecute.

The situation with the tribe reminds me just how important people skills are in the Forest Service. Unlike most forestry-trained district rangers, I had experience with public speaking, mediation, facilitation, and responding to interviews. I think these abilities gave me a leadership advantage. One of my gifts and a strength is that I easily relate to people. They tend to trust me. This is true of all kinds of individuals, no matter their position or stage in life. In this case and many others, my approach was to keep all stakeholders informed. Because of transparency and my clear desire to understand and respect Native history and culture, I secured agreement from several tribes to change their hunting regulations to exclude the monument closure area, and the Suquamish agreed to prosecute the tribal member who killed the elk. I believe this was a far better outcome than federal prosecution.

Disagreements between skiers and snowmobilers presented yet another challenge. Both groups wanted to use the same trails. No accidents had happened yet, but their safety concerned me. The skiers and snowmobilers both loved the mountain, and both groups volunteered regularly to build and maintain trails. Beyond the safety issue, this intergroup competition threatened public/private trail work partnerships and presented a major problem. My workforce could not accomplish the work alone; I just did not have enough employees. These issues made us a major stakeholder, and so I decided to bring both groups together. I would use an interest-based, collaborative problem-solving process that started with talking about the consequences for each of them if our partnerships disintegrated.

Neither group wanted to participate, so I told them the truth: we would be making decisions without their input or closing the trails if they refused. That brought them to the table. When dealing with the public, I had learned the necessity for cooperation and knew that authoritative decision making just made people resent the federal government. These were public lands, and we all had a stake in the outcomes. So, over the course of several meetings and with a lot of compromise, my staff mapped out where each group could go. In turn, I agreed to an additional parking lot for snowmobilers. Hopefully, everyone got something they wanted from the process.

My duties didn't always require hard, time-consuming work. I had learned to have fun in the outdoors, by camping in the wilderness in Montana and Eugene, skiing on the bunny slope at Mount Hood, horseback riding in Eastern Oregon, and golfing in Oakridge—yes, I can include golfing, if we were talking Forest Service business. I remember the first time I went kayaking: I spent two days on the east side of MSH with an organized group of kayakers who had threatened to appeal my decision over a conservation habitat plan for the East Fork of the Lewis River. The plan required putting logs and big rocks into the river to improve spawning and rearing habitat for steelhead, an endangered and threatened species. The group opposed these measures because two kayakers had died because of similar obstructions. The weekend spent with the group was time well spent. They were able to discuss their safety concerns and feel as though someone was listening. We got to know each other better, I was able to explain my obligations under the Endangered Species Act, and this group ultimately worked with my staff about where to put things in the river.

My confidence is based on listening skills, empathy, and humility, coupled with the willingness to go beyond the call of duty to understand and do my job. I attribute these abilities to my journalism degree, which gave me a very different background than most agency managers with degrees in forestry and engineering. Most foresters are trained to think about trees, surveying, and resources, not people. I always strived for honesty and truth. I sometimes made hard and unpopular decisions, but I think the trust I built meant people respected me even when I made choices they hated. My time with the kayak group created trust in me and the Forest Service, paving the way for joint implementation of the habitat project and initiating a long-term partnership. Working with them and my staff allowed us to save salmon and create a safe kayaking experience. That was the sort of thing I loved about my job.

Diversifying Mount St. Helens

The assignment at Mount St. Helens gave me more opportunity than ever before to bring minorities into the workforce, something I found exciting. It takes real commitment by leadership to bring people of color into the Forest Service, and as downsizing took hold of the region, in the 1980s and early 1990s, efforts lagged. I finally had the power to do something about diversity, an issue I saw as important not just for employees, but also for our many thousands of visitors. Most of our visitors were Whites, but we also hosted Blacks, Asians, Native Americans, Latinos, international tourists, and others. I also had mostly white permanent employees, but during the summer months, when visitation was high, I could hire interpreters from other ethnic groups.

Why would I care about hiring people of color? Aside from my personal interest, I believe that representation matters. Representation counts because of the message employees send to the public about belonging. I loved watching children's faces light up when they interacted with people who looked like them or spoke to them in their native language. I knew this feeling intimately because I remembered meeting a black teacher when I was in grade school and realizing that I could grow up and teach or get some other professional job. It gave me hope for a future beyond domestic work, since that's what a lot of black women did, especially in the South. I hoped that when students saw women, people of color, and non-English-language speakers at MSH, they could see themselves as forest rangers or interpreters someday. Young people of all backgrounds should know they have options, and it is harder to believe in open possibilities when everyone you see in positions of power is white.

As a supervisor, I was delighted to work with the cooperative education students, who came in under a special work/school program. Over time, I mentored more than one co-op ed student of color,[7] including a Hispanic student who stayed in my home. Her parents appreciated my willingness to host her, because I made sure she called them weekly. When students felt they had experienced discrimination, I listened, shared, and often suggested ways for them to handle their experiences. As an African American woman, I could understand their feelings. As a long-term Forest Service employee, I could also sometimes provide a different perspective. For example, once a student who had been reprimanded told me that his supervisor was prejudiced. When I checked into his claim, I found the supervisor had reprimanded several white employees for the same things. The supervisor said that yes, he criticized employees, but he also complimented them when they did well or corrected their mistakes. I told this to the student, and two weeks later he excitedly reported that the same supervisor recognized him positively at an all-employee meeting. He felt proud and said he realized his supervisor had simply wanted him to do a good job.

It was easier to recruit people of color for public service work in the interpretive center than for fieldwork in the outdoors, especially since few, if any, lived nearby. That meant less opportunity to diversify the resource-based workforce on the westside. Still, diversity mattered there, too, especially in remote forest districts, where most everyone is alike. With Forest Service trying to hire and incorporate women, people of color, and those with disabilities into the agency throughout the 1980s and 1990s, it became even more important to learn to work together. I knew I could not make people value difference, but I could make sure all employees attended the civil rights trainings the agency provided. I believe that as a nation, we are better off when we learn how little difference there really is between us. A lot of local employees had very little experience with people outside their own racial and cultural groups, so I hoped this exposure to other people helped them better understand the need for inclusion and acceptance, key issues around diversity.

Money Problems

I felt successful in maintaining a more diverse workforce, but keeping up the physical structures and equipment of the interpretive centers presented other challenges. Forest Service had spent millions of dollars building the three centers, and they were always open, except on Thanksgiving, Christmas, and New Year's Day. All of these extremely visible and visited sites had high-tech equipment and interactive displays with significant maintenance costs. The problem was that tech costs grew, while appropriated funds decreased or stayed stagnant. Downsizing employees was hard enough; now I had to find additional funding to maintain the structures and technology. Charging fees helped offset some of the costs, but fee projections depended on many variables: weather, attendance, maintenance costs, and staffing levels. I needed funding for the public service organization component of MSH, and I needed help identifying solutions to my money problems. I needed creative ways to deal with an impending economic crisis.

I've found that problem solving is easier when people work together, so I created a taskforce made up of employees and community members from Castle Rock and other westside communities. We had to set priorities, so we designated which sites to keep open, from trails to visitor centers. With all of the downsizing, we also had to identify key permanent positions; all others would be temporary or volunteer. As we reduced employment and tried to keep services, the need for expanding partnerships emerged. We decided that one of the best ways to get buy-in and assistance was to develop a nonprofit for MSH. Nonprofit ideas had been floating around when I arrived, but my taskforce brought people together, solidified ideas, and shaped an ambitious proposal for an institute for higher learning at our Silver Lake Visitor Center. Partners included federal and state agencies, environmental groups, tribes, local businesses, and the surrounding communities.

A retired USGS employee agreed to work as point person, along with a dedicated group of volunteers. By the time I left MSH, we were moving toward political support for the Mount St. Helens Institute. This far-reaching proposal included asking the University of Washington to provide professors and graduate students to teach, collect, analyze, and interpret data. The overall idea was to turn the visitor center into a center for higher learning, with Washington State and its universities as partners.

We hoped for congressional support to build employee housing across from Silver Lake, much like the agency compounds on districts. We also sought corporate scholarships from Weyerhaeuser. Lastly, we proposed recruiting international students to do research and learn interpretive and environmental education skills.

I was not around to see these bold recommendations carried out, but our work provided a framework for the forest and our partners. The outcome was much smaller than the original plan. I later learned that, in 2000, the Washington State Park system took over the Silver Lake Visitor Center. In 2013 Coldwater Visitor Center operated as an educational facility and conference center in cooperation with the MSH Institute, with a mission "to advance understanding and stewardship of the earth through science, education and exploration of volcanic landscapes."[8] Sadly, the interactive exhibits were removed. Without government funding, volunteers did everything they could to maintain a place for visitors and where groups could hold educational conferences. The big idea was reduced to smaller pieces.

On the Ground at MSH

The eastside work was interesting because of the interpretive centers, but the everyday work of land management played out on the district's westside. Most of the time, people associated the Mount St. Helens District with the interpretive centers in the blast zone, but this single emphasis downplayed the "real" on-the-ground work the Forest Service accomplished on its 110,000-acre district. Like many ranger districts, most westside employees lived and worked close to home and came from nearby communities. These were local folks who knew they would not advance in the agency because they wanted to stay put. The pay was decent, they loved the work, and most knew the location of every road, trail, and campsite on the district. Occasionally, a forester or an engineer who grew up in the area transferred out for a promotion. These individuals were the exception. More cycled into the region, gained experience, and moved on with the opportunity to achieve a higher grade. In all cases, the employee performance was outstanding, just as I experienced in other districts.

One of my major accomplishments at MSH was the management plan we completed for timber, roads, and recreation during my tenure. A management plan identifies all the projects in an entire area. The plan was in process when I arrived, and we finished it so that it would protect a very popular area, the Mount Margaret Backcountry, which had been closed after the blast. We got to work implementing the project, and put in tent pads and composting toilets to make the site accessible. We also limited overnight use and collected fees for use because of the area's land-scape vulnerability due to new plant growth. The extra money paid for backcountry rangers to monitor the site while budgets declined all over the agency, even at MSH. Volunteers and partnerships also helped offset the budget shortfalls. As funds diminished, volunteers implemented field projects alongside paid employees. They gave interpretive talks at the visitor centers, built trails, constructed facilities in our horse camps and snow parks, and even collected data for fish and other research projects.

One of the most important lessons I learned at MSH was that, wherever I went from there, I would need to depend on volunteers and community partnerships. These were good lessons. By the time I left, I had saved more than $500,000 for the unit. I felt good about my tenure, because the agency recognized my work by providing the monument with several awards for implementing cost-saving actions. These were accomplishments I could use on my resume, especially since the next job I applied for would be forest supervisor.

In the meantime, I had other, more personal struggles. One day I got a call about Trina that started our entire family on another grueling jour-ney. It was 1998, and Trina was in the hospital in Arkansas. She was sick, really sick. She had gone to a meeting where some folks had the flu. They recovered, but the virus became life-threatening for Trina. She got myo-carditis, an infection that occurs when a person's body attacks its own immune system and weakens the heart. The myocarditis attacked Trina's left ventricle, making it hard for her body to pump blood to the rest of her body; it also causes heart palpitations, bloating, dizziness, breathlessness, and fatigue. Myocarditis can cause heart failure. It also made it hard for her to work. Trina needed her family. By then, she had worked for Forest Service for two years, first at the Job Corps Center on Mount Hood, then in Little Rock. We talked about it, and with me at Mount St. Helens, alone in a rural district, her coming to Washington State wasn't the answer. She needed to be close to my large family network, so she got a transfer to the WO in DC and went to live with her sister.

Not long afterward, I got my professional wish. It felt surreal when I got my dream job as forest supervisor for the Siuslaw National Forest. I had gone through the usual application process, and when the phone call came from Nancy Graybeal, I nearly had to pinch myself. My combination of joy and disbelief wasn't so much about the promotion or the money (although that mattered a lot!) as it was about the title and the stature. Becoming a forest supervisor is what I had worked for, and for so long. I remember thinking, *Forest supervisors are revered in our agency. Now I am a forest supervisor but I didn't get here the same way as everyone else. Will I be worthy of reverence? This feels unreal.* As I headed back to Corvallis and another coveted job, I was thinking that the hard work had been more than worth it.

CHAPTER 7

Can You See Me Now?

I WAS HEADING BACK TO CORVALLIS, only this time I had truly arrived: I was the first female African American forest supervisor in the nation. I was proud of my tenure at Mount St. Helens, and this new appointment felt like the reward for a job well done. The Eugene *Register-Guard, Corvallis Gazette-Times* and the *Oregonian* newspapers introduced me to my new constituency as a pioneer blazing a trail from Washington, DC, through Montana, Washington State, and Oregon. My position as forest supervisor was new territory not only for me, but also for the Forest Service. We were betting on each other, and the stakes were high. I had watched and participated in the continued unfolding of Mount St. Helens' ecological network, the flora and fauna that brought back an ecosystem. Just as wildlife, birds, and sprouts of green reemerged on the once-barren landscape, I realized that I, too, had blossomed toward my new assignment. I knew my dream job would present huge and unexpected challenges.

This would be a test of my survival as a leader, and of the Siuslaw National Forest and its employees. It was also a test for women of color. There were a few, very few, other black women reaching for high-level positions in the Forest Service. Melody Mobley, a forester, had held a staff position in the WO, but left the agency a few years earlier. Leslie Weldon, a wildlife biologist, also had a staff position in DC. Now, it was 1999, and I was the first black woman to manage an entire national forest—*ever*. Weldon, who later became deputy chief for the National Forest System, followed me the next year as the second African American female forest supervisor—on the Deschutes National Forest. Leslie later said she stood on my shoulders to get there.[1]

And the Siuslaw, with its diverse and productive landscape, was special. The forest includes 630,000 acres, bordered by the Willamette Valley on the east and the Pacific Ocean on the west. As the USFS website describes it, "From forest floor to ocean shore the Siuslaw National Forest stretches from the lush forests of the coastal mountains to the unique Oregon Dunes and the beaches of the Pacific Ocean." The major rivers, the Nestucca, Alsea, Siuslaw, and Umpqua, provide excellent habitat for anadromous fish, while a variety of trees fasten a mountain range buttressed by the sea. The forest extends from Tillamook to Coos Bay, Oregon, and is one of only two national forests in the lower forty-eight states to claim oceanfront property.

The Siuslaw has four major recreation sites, all unique in their own way. The Oregon Dunes area, deemed a national recreation area by Congress in 1972, includes 31,500 acres of "large oblique dunes found . . . nowhere else in the world." Mist shrouds the interface between dunes, forest, and ocean, so close together they are described as "rare and hauntingly beautiful." The forest also hosts my beloved Marys Peak, the 1,076-acre Sand Lake Recreation Area, and Cape Perpetua National Scenic Area.

At Cape Perpetua, forested crag meets the sea, with an eight-hundred-foot-high headland, the topmost viewpoint on the Oregon coast that is reachable by car. Anytime I had a chance to parade my forest to higher-ups, I took them to Cape Perpetua, a place with seventy miles of coastland, where a visitor could see nearly forty miles out to sea on a clear day. The site is so ecologically unique that in the 1960s it became a scenic area, 2,700 acres of temperate rainforest where spruce forest meets the ocean. A Civilian Conservation Corps camp, followed by a World War II camp for conscientious objectors, also left marks on the landscape, from campgrounds to trails to trees planted decades earlier.[2]

The Siuslaw is rich with ecological diversity. As in other Northwest forests, treasured old-growth stands burst with life. From the massive ferns that spring out of the damp ground alive with micro-organisms to huge fungi that hang from dense bark to treetop canopies alive with birds, a variety of species thrives at every level. The forested ecosystem is priceless, and the shoreline ecology is also invaluable. Shorelines, the intertidal sites where land meets water, are some of the most sensitive ecological zones of all, places that are home to unique species with limited habitat. Pools of seawater host a plethora of marine species, starfish, anemones, and barnacles, at the mercy of humans and animals but also of winds and tide. When a tidal pool dries up, it can kill the biota. Rare microorganisms often live in these intertidal zones, part of an invisible food chain that works its way up to sea and land alike. Shoreline vegetation also prevents erosion, while invasions of nonnative grasses contribute to loss of habitat. This delicate system, devoted by Forest Service to public recreation, had to be carefully managed. Driving cars along the beach could be disastrous for natural ecosystems, as could too many visitors. The use of off-road vehicles plagued my tenure.[3]

Clashes on the Siuslaw

The previous Siuslaw forest supervisor, Jim Furnish, had been promoted to deputy chief for national forests in Washington, DC, under Chief Mike Dombeck (1997–2001), formerly the acting director of the BLM. Dombeck returned to Forest Service, where he had earlier served as a fisheries biologist and followed the first non-forester to run the agency, Chief Jack Ward Thomas (1993–1996). It had been a big deal for a wildlife biologist to lead Forest Service in 1993, and it still was. A lot of the old guard resisted the ecosystem-management ideals pioneered by Thomas, but Furnish, who faced problems from decreasing budgets to downsizing to environmentalist challenges, had supported the approach. His own long-term career as a forester and observer of the environmental effects of clear-cutting had convinced him to take steps that matched his ethics, which, in turn, stressed his budget but got him to DC.

In his book, *Toward a Natural Forest,* Jim identified three main challenges that came with declining timber production: "Spotted-owl population declines; then conflicts over the marbled murrelet, a small oceanic bird that nests in big coastal conifers; and finally plummeting salmon stocks." Jim inherited a forest plan that took the allowable timber sale quantity from 320 million board feet (mmbf) to 215 mmbf, but also made cutting mature timber the "highest priority."[4] I saw Jim Furnish as a hero for proclaiming he would not cut old growth on the Siuslaw. He committed to an ecological vision of forest management that many forest supervisors in the region disliked. For most of them, the New Perspectives program, proposed in the early 1990s, followed by the Northwest Forest Plan, and then "ecosystem management" were just words, not the reality of daily, on-the-ground land management. Many forest supervisors still found ways to cut old growth, and Jim received a lot of pushback from his traditionalist peers for halting revenue-producing old-growth cuts. Even his staff resisted. Still, it was clear to me that Jim's sense of ecological responsibility got him out of Region 6, which left this opening for me. By this time, my own land management ethos had developed into a full-blown sense of environmental responsibility. I agreed with Jim's vision and intended to follow it. I had no idea how hard that would be.

One of our concerns was how to achieve a healthier ecosystem at the same time as we underwent staff reductions. Unfortunately, one casualty of downsizing on the Siuslaw included downgrading Jim's GS-15 forest supervisor position to GS-14. This meant a newbie—me—coming in at lower pay, with no backup deputy to show me the ropes, even though I had the same responsibilities as any other forest supervisor. I could have applied for a GS-15 from a GS-13, but there were no such openings at the time. I could have waited for a GS-15 forest supervisor position and stayed on Mount St. Helens, but I received counsel to take this opportunity *now*. If I had to compete with a white male GS-15 forest supervisor, I would be less likely to get the job. If I waited, I'd probably have to go up against traditional foresters who had been in resource management much longer than I had, and who had the "quals." I had the qualifications, but I needed the experience.

The downgraded position meant less cost to the forest, but there was no consequence for Furnish. He moved to a senior executive service (SES) position in the WO, a status ranked in the same category as the chief. The RO (regional office) had a GS-14 recreation staff job opening, and Phil wanted me to take it so I would remain in Portland, but that was not an option for me. I had already been a staff person in the RO and I had a goal: forest supervisor. I wanted it more than I had wanted anything in a long time.

The Price of Ambition

It turned out that my ambition would have more personal costs than I knew. Things had seemed to be looking up, even though Catrina was sick. But not long after I arrived on the Siuslaw, things got worse. Trina had transferred to DC as an analyst for the Smokey Bear and Woodsy Owl programs. Then she met Alan, who became her longtime partner, and decided she really wanted a baby. So, they counseled with an entire board of doctors, who talked with her honestly. They said it wasn't a good idea, that they didn't think she would make it through a pregnancy. "It could end up with you needing a new heart or problems with the baby," they said. Trina considered this carefully, and then decided to take her chances. She did okay through the first part of the pregnancy, but the end did not go well. At seven months pregnant, Trina walked into the WO Forest Service building as an employee for her last time. She had to go on bedrest until Alana, my beautiful baby granddaughter, was ready for birth.

Alana was born prematurely on March 12, 2000. I headed to DC right away when Trina went into labor, and by the time I arrived, she was in the operating room. She had gone into heart failure while having the baby. My uncle was with her when she went in, and he told me Trina had left a message: "Don't worry, Mommy, if I don't come out, I will be okay, because it's God's will." Trina has a deep faith, and that's how she saw it. I was worried.

Thank God, she made it. Little Alana went into neonatal ICU because she was born with fluid on the brain. It was three weeks before they could let her go. I had stayed there to help her daddy with the baby, but had to leave before Trina came home. You can imagine how hard that was! Trina was in the ICU for another week, and went home on medication and with restrictions for her heart. That June, on Father's Day, her symptoms got worse. She went to the hospital, and this time they said the medication wasn't enough. She needed a transplant. They put her on a defibrillator, and two weeks later the new heart came, on August 15, 2000. Alana was five months old. It was a hellish summer.

Catrina hasn't worked since then, not just because of her own health issues,[5] but also because it turned out that the fluid on Alana's brain didn't dry up as the doctors had predicted. It wasn't until Alana started walking that we knew something was wrong. She was about a year old when Trina, Nicki, and Alan learned that Alana had epilepsy. She would stare into space; we just thought it was a baby staring, but she was having mini-seizures. By that time, I had been in Corvallis for about a year, working my dream job and contending with other kinds of hard issues. None of them matched the possible loss of my daughter. But they did tap into long-standing regional tensions, made stronger by the law.

A Perfect Storm

Jim's groundbreaking success in ecological management left the watersheds of the Siuslaw in better condition than he found them. But the employees were in worse shape, not just there but everywhere, left behind on forests with decreased budgets, without financial support to do their work. Significant downsizing happened on the Siuslaw just before I arrived, and further cuts hit as I came on the scene. This was a perfect storm of colliding factors that I knew would make it difficult to successfully continue Jim's legacy. Furnish recognized the unpredictable challenges in protecting the spotted owl and salmon. He and I both had to ask, How can we follow guidelines for ecosystem management with so many traditionalist attitudes inside the agency, a timber industry pushing for massive cuts, and a budget that privileges harvests over habitat?

Forest Service is supposed to operate based on science, but there is an inherent contradiction in its funding and management. You would think, in the environmental age, that sustainable forestry would drive funding allocations from Congress. But no, the government distributes money based on timber harvest numbers. That's why Region 6 raked in the money in the 1980s. Revenues determined our budgets, something I had to contend with in trying to get work done on the ground. No one talks about this flaw when it comes to ecological goals. Another factor affects forest management: who the president is. Jim managed the Siuslaw under President Bill Clinton, who took charge soon after the spotted owl went on the Endangered Species list in 1990.

A year later, Judge William Dwyer placed an injunction on all timber sales in spotted owl habitat. This led to court battles among environmentalists, industry, and Forest Service, prompting President Clinton to call for a Pacific Northwest Forest Summit in 1993. This intervention led to the Northwest Forest Plan (NWFP), meant to coordinate efforts to sustainably manage forests. Timber harvests continued, but at levels nowhere near those earlier periods. The Siuslaw, which sold about eleven billion board feet of timber between 1960 and 1990, had possibly been one of the most intensively cut in a forest of its size. By the early 1980s, damage to soil, rivers, and fish habitat halted timber sales on the Mapleton District, the very place I had researched when in the WO.[6] Other sales were stopped all around the region in light of the spotted owl ruling.

The Northwest Forest Plan had reduced the Siuslaw's allowable sale quantity from 213 million board feet to 23 mmbf by creating three distinct ecological zones. Two of the zones hosted very diverse biological communities and sensitive populations. The late successional reserves (LSRs) were forested areas alive with organisms and wildlife like the spotted owl and the marbled murrelet, and stands on their way to becoming old growth. Riparian, or streamside, zones four to five hundred feet wide protected terrestrial and aquatic habitats—often the home of endangered salmon. Neither LSRs nor riparian zones allowed commercial harvests. Timber cutting was allowed in the third zone, the matrix, which made up only 6 percent of the Siuslaw's land base.[7] The final blow to timber harvests came when staff realized that they had only one available mature timber stand; all other stands housed owls and murrelets. The thriving timber program could not continue on the Siuslaw, the nation's beautiful, lush, coastal rainforest, rife with wood.

I arrived on the Siuslaw with a Republican president in office, George W. Bush, who supported industry's timber harvest goals. Couple this with communities dependent on timber jobs to support schools and other local public services like libraries, and by 1999 national forests were in a real pickle—low harvests, fewer revenues, and conflict between industry and environmentalists. The agency responded to these issues by pushing for community and public/private partnerships, doing "more with less," and creating a formal partnership program. While large numbers of people lost their jobs at the forest and district levels, the agency hired a GS-14 partnership program person for the WO and in the RO. Downsizing and partnerships were not new to me. I knew that working with the public would be the key to accomplishing anything, and I also needed to sit down with the environmentalists responsible for the injunction.

I had inherited a budget deficit, declining personnel, and the westside injunction, which halted *all* cutting, not just old growth. Mine was one of nine national forests affected. Judge Barbara Rothstein had declared that Forest Service and BLM had not complied with NWFP mandates intended to protect endangered and threatened species. Collectively, Rothstein said, because surveys to identify harmful conditions weren't completed properly, there was "a discrete and immediate harm posed" to salmon and steelhead. This meant that millions of board feet of timber could not be sold,[8] which affected both local communities and forest funding. And me. I began to fear I had taken on a sinking ship. I also wondered, *If I fail at this job, will it make it harder for African American women who come after me?* I didn't have a playbook, so I knew I had to be smart and make things up along the way.

Working Together

After the NWFP, Jim had turned to thinning harvestable wood in areas of past clear-cuts, a practice called salvage logging. My job was to use what Furnish had started and add it to my own record. I was a nontraditional selection and did not always speak the party line (timber). I was a black woman who did not necessarily think like some of my white male counterparts, and I knew my empathy for people and places didn't always align with typical agency behavior. Still, I had to try to do something. These clear-cut areas were often so densely covered with downed brush and other debris that they presented a fire hazard and wildlife couldn't use them, aside from a few deer munching at twilight. Massive amounts of wood lay on the ground, along with overstocked stands of second-growth timber. I needed to harvest it, so I could address my budget issues, but I also reconfirmed with the employees, the RO, environmentalists, industry and the public at large that, like Furnish, I would not cut any old growth, even if the injunction lifted.

I led with this when I asked Oregon Wild and other environmental groups[9] to support me in getting out from under the injunction by continuing the practice of second-growth thinning for harvestable wood. I told them I would listen to all stakeholders, the environmental groups, the Siuslaw community, and my employees. I asked them to give me a chance to work together. "You don't know me," I said, and "I want to be honest. In all fairness, this means I will have to listen to industry too." But, "I believe in the agency's ecosystem management principles." Finally, I asked them to look at my earlier Forest Service and BLM accomplishments before they judged me. I believed my past work spoke to my integrity. I just needed a chance.

Fortunately, the environmental organizations decided to support me. Since we weren't cutting old growth in the first place, they agreed to ask the judge to take the Siuslaw off the injunction and the appeal. My successful negotiation with the plaintiffs suing the Forest Service started us on a path toward honest and trusting negotiations. I still think that maybe a positive relationship with environmentalists throughout the region could have led to less conflict all around. But it had been a long haul for the agency, one that had required a cognitive shift in how land managers viewed their jobs. Even with the "ologists" regularly weighing in, most leaders still saw environmentalists as the enemy.

Now we could start planning and implementing projects on the Siuslaw, but it would take augmenting my declining budget. Everyone in the agency respects the fact that forest supervisors manage thousands of acres, sometimes millions. We also supervise a lot of people and are held responsible for results on the ground. We are often venerated. The WO and RO make rules and policies, but forest supervisors provide the leadership that improves watersheds, creates healthy fish and wildlife habitat, and provides recreational opportunities for millions of people. Despite this, I knew it would be useless to talk with the timber staff in the RO about more money for my forest. Our refusal to cut the big trees put us at the bottom of the barrel for funding allocations. Not only do old-growth trees produce a lot of wood, they are durable, rot resistant, and the main moneymaker for industry and for timber and recreation programs. My dilemma was how to maintain my forest's budget in these conditions. It would take time to find partners and volunteers to assist us. In the meantime, I had to make sure our budget from the RO could last until I found ways to increase funding. When Furnish announced that the Siuslaw would no longer cut old growth, he sealed the forest's fate of a deceasing timber budget. With the westside injunction in place regionally, money was even harder to come by than before. I had to do something. I decided to go see Margaret Peterson, the partnership program manager, to try to get more money.

Margaret and I had known each other for a long time. My daughter Catrina babysat for her when Margaret had small children, so we started with a hello and hugs. Then I said, "Margaret, I need your help." She knew about my promotion to the Siuslaw. She also knew I needed money for my forest. I told her what was happening, that no staff in the RO would give me more money, and I hadn't had time to establish volunteers and partners. I said, "Margaret, I need dollars, because my program of work is underfunded." Margaret had just received a partnership proposal from Ecotrust, a nonprofit that seeks environmental solutions in the Northwest through public/private partnerships. Their proposal said they were "excited about the potential of working with the Forest Service and its many partners." I got lucky.

Ecotrust encouraged the Forest Service to apply for grant funding, and Margaret agreed to recommend the Siuslaw. This was great news, because I knew the Siuslaw could meet any criteria needed to qualify. Ecotrust supported an environmental position that precluded major timber harvests, and so did we. By coming under Ecotrust and the RO umbrella, I became eligible for other funds for ecosystem management, the buzzword for where there was money, in wildlife for example. I found financing to supplement my budget and get work done on the ground with the help of partnerships like this. Margaret helped a struggling forest supervisor to realize her goals and objectives, and to this day I am very grateful.

My goal was to improve watersheds within the coast range. In 2001, a year after my arrival, the Siuslaw published my vision for the forest for decades to come. In the business plan, titled "Decades of Change . . . A Challenge for the Future," I wrote, "Our restoration projects will have measurable and evident outcomes. Outcomes that emphasize species and habitat recovery across entire watersheds."[10] I wanted results on the ground, and I knew my staff could produce them. They were smart and innovative, educated and informed. I trusted them and made decisions based on their recommendations. I also focused on finding contracts and jobs in rural communities.

I decided that we had to increase the acres thinned in the overstocked second-growth forests. My staff also committed to appropriating funds for completing connected work on private land. We worked tirelessly with our partners to ensure regional and national recognition of our watershed restoration work on the Siuslaw. We also created the second largest fee demonstration program in Oregon and Washington. Ours had been the first forest to collect fees for special forest products, woodcutting, and other activities on national forest land. We needed the revenue.

When we delivered revenue from our projects, the RO recaptured funds for our budget. I credit my recreation staff officer for working with the rangers to secure those funds for reinvestment. The way Forest Service funding works is that ranger districts are funded last. The WO and RO take their money to support work and staff. Then, they divvy it up to forest supervisors, who decide on ranger district funding; I kept as little of that money for operations as possible. I didn't try to increase my staff. I supported the staff I had by giving them what they needed for projects as they saw fit. The recreation staff put money back into the district. By maintaining operational levels, rather than trying to grow, we had more money to get the work done.

Stewardship and Strategy

Our stewardship pilot program meant money coming in to the forest that enabled us to do work enhancing clean water and clean air and improving wildlife and fish habitat. Getting projects planned and implemented in coastal Oregon was sometimes contentious and time-consuming. I had to work with groups from the Association of Forest Service Employees for Environmental Ethics (AFSEEE) to local business owners who felt strongly about how the forest should be managed. It was *their* national forest. Some issues were local in scope and some were so controversial they ended up in the WO. Even an easy project could be taken out of a supervisor's hands by the WO. The more controversial the issue—like putting a trail or logging road into a roadless area—the more likely the national office was to get involved. Lucky me—a recent storm had created an issue with blowdown: logs and debris were strewn over dozens of acres in a roadless area north of the economically depressed community of Coos Bay. The storm had also hit neighboring Weyerhaeuser's property to the east—private land.

With acres and acres of untouched downed wood, community members clamored for us to do something. Environmentalists said to leave it alone. The scenario got worse when I learned that Weyerhaeuser had started salvage logging on their land, and the county had an in-holding within the blowdown area. Worse yet, the county was building a road to salvage their blowdown, because they had an easement that predated the roadless-area designation. The community and local politicians called for Forest Service to also salvage logs within the roadless area.

I worried this could be one of those tough issues that the national office would want to take over. If I authorized salvage logging, environmentalists would take me straight to court, and my decision would automatically go to the regional office and maybe to the WO for the final decision. All of this would require a lot of time and money. My problem was that the WO did not understand local sensitivities. I knew I had to be strategic: we started working with stakeholders, talking through their issues, and we visited the site several times. My personal opinions aligned with the environmentalists: Why touch it? But this was not about me.

Many stakeholders agreed that the integrity of the roadless area had already been compromised. Weyerhaeuser was already logging, and the county was building a road to their lands, no matter what I said. Then there was the fire hazard to the adjacent community with all that downed wood. We also considered the economic situation in Coos Bay. The community wanted the tax revenue from timber sales, and they needed it. If we wanted to harvest the downed timber, we needed to write an environmental assessment agreeable to all. Ultimately, working with all sides, we published an EA in May without appeal. We sold the salvage in July, stipulating the company must use local workers. The contract was implemented in October. I felt good about how industry, environmentalists, and the community came together to do the right thing for the roadless area. There was no recognition from the RO.

Meanwhile, downsizing kept rearing its ugly head, as it did for Heceta Head Lighthouse on the Oregon coast. The lighthouse was a valuable asset; however, Ranger Doris Tai could no longer afford to manage the maintenance and staff. I remember thinking, *Here I go, Mount St. Helens all over again.* On MSH, we had looked at the National Park Service and state parks to consider more efficient site management. So, we decided to ask whether NPS was interested in the lighthouse, and we sought input from the RO and the community. The National Park Service turned us down.

We then came up with a risky idea. I had concluded, after Mount St. Helens, that sometimes the best practice is to turn government business over to an eager entrepreneur or agency. We proposed contracting the lighthouse out under the Granger-Thye Act of 1950, which authorized us to permit lands under our purview. Our proposal identified interpretation and building maintenance services as the obligations of the lessee. Under Granger-Thye, the government receives 17 percent of all revenue, plus the cost of administering the permit. We had a lot of responses to our solicitation, and we selected a couple who turned the lighthouse into a bed and breakfast.

While I was on the Siuslaw, this couple doubled the number of lighthouse employees (many from the community) and completed the restoration. They booked reservations for the B&B as many as three years out, and several travel magazines included articles about the lighthouse. Their success enabled them to expand to special events such as weddings and retirement parties, with promotional packages that now include a la carte photographers, catered meals, and other special perks. The best part of the deal was subcontracting the services from local businesses. Reservations were also available via internet. Three years earlier, we had been faced with shutting down the lighthouse; as I left the forest, the B&B turned a profit. Waldport Ranger Doris Tai did the heavy lifting, I rewarded her, and the RO rewarded me.

Downsizing had pushed us to innovate with the lighthouse, but when it came to actual land management work, losing employees was tough. I had a wonderful staff. George Burns was the ranger at Hebo near Tillamook; Doris Tai at Waldport, near Yachats; Bill Helphinstine was the Mapleton ranger; and Ed Becker was ranger for the Oregon Dunes in Reedsport. My staff included Mary Zuslage, resources; Mike Harvey, recreation; Doug McDonald, engineering; Woody Fine, administration; Bob Vanderlinden, administration; Sue Olson and Joni Quarnstrom, both public affairs; Maria Nelson, civil rights; Paul Burns, fish biologist; Karen Barnett, hydrologist; and Dale Edwards, my secretary and gatekeeper. Dale planned all my meetings, kept my calendar, organized paperwork for signature in the order of priority, and served as my sounding board. All or some of these individuals are part of my story on the Siuslaw. They did the work behind the many awards I received.

The need to do more with less had begun under Jim Furnish, but Jim did not have to deal with sharing staff—that came after I arrived. The RO pushed for the Willamette and Siuslaw to implement this, and it quickly became a reality. This dictate affected me and my staff and later my four ranger districts. Willamette forest supervisor Darrel Kenops and

I met to determine which staff to share. We agreed to share Mary Zuslage as resource staff for both forests. We would share Doug McDonald
in engineering, Woody Fine in administration, and Sue Olson, public
affairs. When we combined staff, Joni Quarnstrom was put under Sue,
and Bob Vanderlinden eventually retired. Sharing staff was the epitome of
"doing more with less." It saved money for the region because both forests
contributed to salaries, but it was hard on the people doing the work.
They had to commute between two forests, complete a program of work
for both, and supervise staff at two sites. Scheduling meetings and field
trips sure was complicated. The Willamette benefited, though. By sharing
Mary, the Siuslaw could make up the shortfall on their allowable timber
harvest. There was not a lot of fanfare regarding the Siuslaw bailing out
the mighty Willamette, but I saw pride and joy on the faces of my staff.

Community Challenges and Politics

Some of our important constituencies included politicians, and one of our
favorites was Governor Barbara Roberts. We knew she supported ecosystem management, so we took her on show-me trips so she could see how
things worked on the ground. I remember escorting her and some of our
partners to talk about what a timber sale in second growth would look
like. She was very happy to hear about our future projects. Governor Roberts was not the only official I met with. Once a year, forest supervisors
went to Washington, DC, to meet with their congressional delegations.
We spent some time with Senator Mark Hatfield and his chief of staff
while there. I had met the senator once, in a lunch at the University Club.
I wasn't intimidated, but I didn't feel like I was part of the conversation, or
could be, without someone bringing me into it. That didn't happen. When
we went to his DC office, Senator Hatfield stayed long enough to thank us
for our service, but we made our presentation to his chief of staff. Maybe
he was just busy, but the senator's exit made me think that innovative
approaches to forest management didn't interest him. What I know is that
because of his advocacy for logging, industry loved Senator Hatfield, as
did people in rural communities—environmentalists and ecologists, not
so much. Our experience with Congressman Peter DeFazio was different.
Not only did he stay for our presentation, he already knew specifics about

some of our projects. Like Governor Roberts, the congressman visited the Siuslaw for a show-me trip. We had earned his support.

I really had trouble with one Lane County commissioner, Anna Morrison, who seemed to view me in a different light. She wanted to make sure the taxpayers' money was spent efficiently, something I agreed with. She also took a hard stand on timber sales, knowing they supported jobs and schools in her community. I understood that, and I wanted to build a positive relationship with her. But I quickly realized that she was suspicious, even challenging, of almost everything I did. I tried building open communication by going to her, especially when a big project loomed. I knew a face-to-face relationship was as important with her as with the environmentalists, and I didn't understand her animosity. Without saying it, her hostile body language told me, "I don't like you, Gloria." I have no idea why she was so dismissive and combative. Industry didn't shout about my projects and ideas, and they seemed less aggressive than the commissioner. I didn't think she had that kind of relationship with Jim, so I asked around. I wanted to build trust between us.

What I found was something I had never had to deal with before: a staff member going behind my back and saying things to the commissioner about me. Honestly, this really hurt me. This person had known the commissioner personally for years. They were friends, lived in the same community, went to the same church, and his district resource staff person even babysat for the commissioner's children sometimes. I had never been naïve about relationships. They matter in order to support the work; that was the bottom line. Agency relationships should get the work done and make the outcomes even better. Did I listen like I said I would? Was I honest? Did I make concessions when their input made sense? I had no time to dwell on anything but my job. Did I think about their impression of me? Did they see me as just a woman, a black woman, someone who grew up on the East Coast? If I thought about these things at all, I brushed them away. I had no time for such nonsense.

But leaders expect loyalty from their staff. Employees may talk among themselves, but rarely did a leader anticipate or accept sabotage from their staff with outside individuals. I never would have guessed that this ranger was repeating almost every conversation I had with my leadership team to the commissioner. Despite this, I would not change how I moved forward with my program of work and communications with the team. Commissioner Morrison continued to challenge me on all fronts.

The strain between us increased when the RO directed all forests supervisors to work with local commissioners and form a six-person community-based board of citizens. These boards would determine how to use the forest's timber sale receipts. We could allocate funds only for ecosystem projects on the ground, not for general operations or even processes like meetings, show-me trips, or preparing maps or EAs. The board would decide which conservation projects to address. Each board should include three individuals from industry and three environmentalists, recommended by the commissioners to me, the forest supervisor. I could accept or veto their suggestions, but they could not veto mine. Still, I knew that meeting summaries would show veto actions, which meant I couldn't reject the proposals. Working with the commissioners took precedence over halting nominations, even if I didn't like them.

Putting that board together really brought me head-to-head with Commissioner Morrison. I also knew that she wanted to stack the board with conservatives, whose ideas about forest management privileged timber harvest rather than healthy forests, so I decided to be strategic. I accepted all of her nominations until we got to the last pick. Earlier that week, I had called Andy Stahl, the AFSEEE guy who followed Jeff DeBonis, and asked him to attend our meeting. I knew Andy was a good orator and could hold his ground against any industry person. Chalk one up for the good guys! I rejected only the last nominee, and proposed Andy as my final decision. There would be five conservatives and Andy, who had a region-wide reputation for speaking out about bad practices on national forests. I knew I needed a strong environmentalist like him on the board. There would be no more nominations, votes, or discussions. This board would decide how we could use the funds. I believed that by working with the board, the commissioners, and the community we could make good things happen on the ground. My choice did not improve my relationship with the commissioner, but my staff supported it and remained highly motivated.

Great Things Happening

We were doing important work. We thinned dense second-growth forest to establish ecological conditions for future old growth. We closed roads, took out dikes, and put back meandering streams for fish habitat. One of our watershed partners, Johnny Sandstrom, became a critical voice between the forest and his community. We worked on several rivers in the Siuslaw Basin, but Johnny worked with us on one of the most memorable, the Karnowsky Creek project, a tributary of the Siuslaw River. Mary Zuslage supervised Paul Burns and Karen Bennett, the fish biologist and hydrologist, respectively, who spearheaded this project. Mary did a great job on both forests! At Karnowsky, we took what we knew about stream ecology and pushed even further by essentially recreating the path and shape of the original creek. We used old maps and photos to create a masterfully done painting, a scenario of what we hoped Karnowsky Creek and the Siuslaw River would look like five years out. Then, my staff and contractors dug a ditch to restore the original pathway of the creek. Our unprecedented, meandering design mimicked the creek's historical shape, and we hoped this experimental method would return fish to the stream.

Staff and I discussed the challenges of this kind of innovative work. If anyone else was doing this in the region, we weren't aware of it. We kept the community and our partners close, held regular meetings, and brought in maps and aerial views of the creek to share. The project was overwhelmingly successful. Fish started coming back immediately. Recently planted poplars provided shade, and the boulders we put in eventually created resting pools and cover for fish. I am proud to say that this work in the Siuslaw Basin received international attention. Nobody had completely dug out a stream and restored its meandering flow. Our river was one of five nominated for the prestigious Thiess International Riverprize from the International RiverFoundation—the only nomination from the United States! We did not win that year, but the forest won in June 2005, the year after I moved on. I was disappointed that the regional forester did not visit the forest while I was there.

Great things happened on the Siuslaw because I had so many extremely bright employees who weren't afraid to think creatively and try new challenges. I also took risks that paid off. I happily received the agency's nationwide Rise to the Future Line Officer of the Year award in 2003. The RO must have nominated me for the work we did on the forest.

I appreciated the recognition but wished there had been some monetary reward, too. Over the years, I'd seen guys get monetary awards left and right. Even though I did not receive as many of these financial awards as I thought I should, I still gave them to my staff all the time. It never felt like we got a lot of kudos from inside the agency, but we received recognition from our communities, other agencies, and our partners. I felt really good when Bill Possiel, president of the National Forest Foundation and one of our partners, asked me to join him at a national meeting in Washington, DC. Congress chartered this nonprofit foundation in 1993, with a simple goal that appealed to me: "Bring people together to restore and enhance our National Forests and Grasslands." Bill wanted me to think about joining the board.[11]

I knew Bill from show-me trips on the Siuslaw. He clearly appreciated our partnership work and results. I remember feeling like a fish out of water at that meeting in DC, as I looked around to see regional foresters up and down the table. Neither of us knew, but Bill and I learned that day—the board was made up only of regional foresters! *Oh well*, I thought, *I have enough to do already!* I went home smiling and thinking about the many times I'd watched a meeting like this from the outside. *Now I am at the table; in fact, I'm at a lot of tables.* That was good enough for me.

Bill's recognition satisfied me. Others were silent, but I stood on their shoulders: Tom Hamilton, Arlen Roll, Barbara Ingersoll, Mike Kerrick, Bev McCulley, and Karen Tressler, to name just a few. I also stood on the shoulders of Jim Furnish. I based my plans on the vision Jim had left behind. This is what we do; a leader comes in and takes up where his or her predecessor left off, or starts with a new vision. Jim's work got him a senior executive service (SES) job in the Washington office. Mine got me a GS-15; I applied for SES, but was turned down. As I recall, Gary Larson, GS-15 on the Mount Hood NF, got the SES training. I didn't get feedback regarding my application, so I decided that maybe GS-14s, even forest supervisors, need not apply. I was not bitter, but some feedback would have been nice. After all, I had demonstrated my willingness to work for anything the agency put in front of me. I guess I did not get to my GS-15 soon enough to take the next step, but it was a great consolation prize. I could do SES another day. I would have to wait and see.

Challenges for the Future

I left the Siuslaw with accomplishments that moved us toward ecologically sustainable watersheds. My staff and I had carved a clear path to the future. Our large cadre of partners from the community and other agencies also contributed to our success. Our accomplishments and more were highlighted the year I left, in the forest's 2004 Monitoring and Evaluation Report, which included my earlier statement about "measurable and evident outcomes" and took me beyond pride by showing I'd kept those promises. I had been there just over five years, and during that time we had restored and protected watersheds, decommissioned culverts, closed roads, and increased fish runs. Higher coho, cutthroat, and steelhead fish counts proved our success. I can't say enough about how proud this African American woman was when she thought about how far she had come! I had moved from a clerical employee to a leader making monumental changes in my agency. I also think I left the Siuslaw in better shape than I found it.

As I prepared to leave, I reflected on my time there. I started with a dire situation for the forest and ended with a national and international legacy that never could have happened without my great innovative employees and our many partnerships. Leaving the place where I did the kind of forest management that encompassed my goals and values was difficult. It was also hard to leave my staff and our many partners, the true conservation heroes. I knew that I could not have passed on the Siuslaw basin in such good shape without them. Our watersheds were living, breathing, changing systems. A lot of work remained, but the forest was set for its next decade.

As I left, I wondered if my organization could really see me now—as a land manager who was as good as, if not better than, some of the men who automatically received recognition and awards; or did they think, *She was just doing her job*? Who knows, maybe they didn't think about it at all. No matter, I had received national and international recognition, and now I had a promotion to GS-15! I thought about how my agency treated men compared with women. I loved the Forest Service, and I was grateful for my career, but I couldn't help reflecting on how I'd been treated by the BLM versus the Forest Service. I had received more recognition for a job well done during my four years with the BLM than in twenty-nine years with Forest Service. Championed by Elaine Zielinski at BLM, I received a Certificate of Appreciation and Superior Service, with monetary compensation. I had only twice before received that sort of recognition in Forest Service, once on Mount St. Helens and again on the Siuslaw. It took five years on the Siuslaw and an international award for Forest Service to take notice. I was glad for the recognition, but I no longer cared. My work on the Siuslaw paved the way to new projects for them and for me. I kept and made new partnerships, and the results showed for decades to come. Our watershed restoration work was so innovative that Jim Furnish commented on it in his own memoir, having taken note from the perspective of the WO that I had kept my promise to strengthen the forest's ecology.

The employees, my partners, and I had done a phenomenal job to get me here. Our accomplishments over my past three leadership jobs proved what I'd always known: that if I took a job I would succeed awesomely. I knew how to communicate with the agency now, and I understood them, even if they did not always appreciate me. I realized that I no longer needed the agency to recognize me exactly as it did the men. Yes, I wondered if they could see me, really see me, as one of them—but they didn't, and I knew it, because the men still didn't seem to value my input. But I'd shown them I belonged, whether they liked it or not. Any questions I had about my own abilities were completely gone. My self-esteem was high. I was good at my job. I had self-confidence, and *I could see me.* The people on the ground could see me, and I realized that was more important than recognition from my peers. I'd come to the end of the road in trying to present myself as worthy of the kind of kudos I'd seen bestowed on men. The organization hadn't changed. The same systems of exclusion remained. This was still Forest Service. But I had broken ground. I had proved to myself not only that I could do the job, but also that I could and did excel. I was excited for the future!

A lot of times, as a forest supervisor nears retirement, they transfer to a desired location for their last assignment. I had been with the agency for nearly thirty years, and I loved it on the Siuslaw. I would have stayed there forever and retired in Oregon, but a GS-15 meant a lot to my financial situation. So, I headed off to the Los Padres National Forest in California just as my two grown daughters and their families moved back to Oregon from Washington, DC. They would be closer but still too far away; yet, my children supported my choice. They said, "Mom, you have worked really hard to get to this place. You need to continue with the work that will be your legacy."

I remember, the day I left the Siuslaw, I told my son that grown dads don't cry. He responded by telling me, "It will be like Montana, and I won't be there to protect you." I smiled and told them that I knew if I ever needed them, they were just a phone call away. "I know you'll come see about me in a heartbeat." We hugged and I got in my car and started the drive to my new office in Goleta, California, another small town in a different state. As I moved down the coast, basking in its spectacular beauty and landscapes, I decided to leave my ghosts where they belonged: behind me.

CHAPTER 8

Breech Birth

A BABY'S BIRTH IS IN SOME WAYS ANALOGOUS to a Forest Service career. Babies are usually born in nine months. I gestated in the Washington, DC, office for twelve years. Many Forest Service careers start at the district level of the organization; a baby starts in the womb, grows, and then heads into the birth canal. A high-level Forest Service career usually moves from the district toward the forest level, then to a regional office, and lastly to birth in the WO. As babies continue to grow outside the womb, so do Forest Service careers grow while moving around the agency.

My career did not resemble a typical birth into the Forest Service. I think of it as a breech birth: I jumped into the Forest Service backward, feet first instead of head first. I guess you could say this is what I did by starting out in the WO and moving from there to Missoula, Montana. My next stop was Portland, Oregon, then Silver Lake, and Eugene. After that, I returned to school and lived in Corvallis. From Oregon State University I moved to Oakridge, and then to Baker City, Oregon, with the BLM. That stint took me back to Washington, DC. After a short time, I moved back to the Pacific Northwest to Amboy, Washington, for a few years before returning to Corvallis. My major moves in terms of national forest administration were from the WO to the RO to the forest-level supervisor's office to the district, and then back to the SO. I began in the WO, the place some people strive to reach by the end of their careers. It took me twenty-five years to get to my first forest supervisor position, but I had a goal and I achieved it.

I had no desire to go back to or to end my career in the WO. I looked forward to retirement in the Pacific Northwest. Nicki, Trina, Andre, and his wife were all near Portland. I had three smart and beautiful grand-daughters, and one intelligent, athletic grandson to spend the rest of my life with. I looked forward to going to volleyball and basketball games, piano recitals, and birthday parties. Which brings me to my last assignment. I was promoted to a GS-15 on the Los Padres National Forest in 2004. I loved California but knew I couldn't afford to retire there. I remember thinking maybe I could get a GS-15 job in the Portland RO in a few years. That would be a wonderful end to a great career, and Phil would no longer have to travel to Southern California. I hadn't done badly for someone who started as a GS-3 dictating machine transcriber. But first, I had to succeed on the Los Padres National Forest.

The Forest Service and Fire

The Siuslaw was one of two national forests in the lower forty-eight states with oceanfront property—the Los Padres is the other. The Siuslaw has 630,000 acres; the Los Padres National Forest runs along the California coast from Ventura to Monterey and heads inland, wrapping up at 1.95 million acres, 88 percent public lands, the rest privately owned in-holdings. To prepare for my work there, I read about the forest, from the recovery of the California condor to the ten wildernesses that make up 48 percent of the land base. The forest has two huge sanctuaries, places few people go. It is home for lots of wildlife: bald eagles, black bears, peregrine falcons, mountain lions, and little critters like raccoons and quail. Forest vegetation includes chaparral and coniferous forests, with around 18,900 acres of old growth. The forest also has a lot of mountain ranges: the Santa Lucia, the Sierra Madre, and the San Rafael, to name a few. I remember thinking that it would take me years to see the entire forest. So much to do and so little time.

As always, my first day on the job stands out, but this one would have been unforgettable no matter what. I was driving to my new office in Goleta, next door to Santa Barbara, when I got a call on my cell phone from the undersecretary of agriculture, Mark Rey. He wanted to know the status of the fire that was threatening the Reagan's Rancho del Cielo at that very moment. The advantage of being a seasoned forest supervisor was that I knew it was okay to tell him the truth. I said that I was heading to my first day at the office and I would get back to him before the day's end. When I hung up, I contacted my new deputy forest supervisor, Gene Blankenship, and asked him to call and update the undersecretary.

The staff was prepared to give me an extensive briefing as soon as I arrived. They had been anxious to meet the new forest supervisor, but the fire, only 10 percent contained, still blazed, and had burned more than a thousand acres. I can't believe I don't remember the name of my first major fire, but I do remember the threat to the Reagan Ranch. Luckily, this fire moved away from the ranch. The acting forest supervisor had called in a Type 2 team, and I was scheduled to visit the fire the next day where the incident commander would brief me. That first overview included the number of people working the fire, identification of the incident commander, and a review of the options if the fire got bigger and I had to call for a Type 1 overhead team.

The Forest Service uses fire complexity analysis to determine its response to conflagrations. We go through a detailed list of questions about conditions, examining things like nearby infrastructure, natural and cultural concerns, fire proximity to other structures, fuel levels, and fire behavior. This information helps the administrator and the incident commander determine the proper response, depending on fire complexity and magnitude. We have to decide things like, How many fire trucks will we need? How many personnel? Should we call someone outside of the Forest Service to help? Our responses are guided by knowledge of the five types of fires.

A Type 5 incident has the lowest level of complexity: it can usually be put out quickly with only five to six district staff. My fire knowledge and experience came from fires on the Siuslaw and my training in Montana, all Type 5 incidents. When fires started on the moist, coastal Siuslaw, my people quickly put them out. No harm, no foul, and our ecosystem stayed unharmed—all good news for a forest supervisor.

A Type 4 incident, such as the one I had just walked into, still uses local resources, but they are shared. You need more engines and more people putting water on that fire than in a Type 5, so one district sends their fire trucks and staff to another district's fire. These short fires last one burning period, which means up to twenty-four hours. They are pretty easily contained by putting a ring of dirt around the fire and removing all brush to keep it from spreading, and then extinguishing the flames inside the circle. The fire might keep smoldering for a while, so before removing resources, staff stay in place to make sure it won't start up again and spread.

A Type 3 fire is too big for a single district to handle, even with help. It exceeds the twenty-four-hour burning period, and the supervisor's office gets more involved—that's me. The SO fire chief, almost always a man, becomes incident commander and calls the shots on how to put out the fire. In this type of fire, the district firefighters and engineers remain on the team and all staff at the SO, from the archaeologist to the public affairs officer, may be activated. That's why all Forest Service employees must be trained in fighting wildfire.

We talk about fire in the Forest Service in terms of attacks, because that's what we do: we strike back. The supervisor's office and districts can manage anything from initial attack (the first twenty-four hours) to an extended attack beyond that first burning period. The incident commander takes time away from the fire every day to formally brief me, to let me know if he needs additional resources, such as an information specialist to communicate with the public. A forest supervisor cannot continue using a Type 3 organization if the fire goes up to the next complexity level.

Type 2 and Type 1 incidents burn for multiple operation periods, meaning days or even weeks, with more acres and all resources, including homes and structures, at stake. If a Type 2 fire increases its intensity and damage, we prepare a second complexity analysis and a written action plan commensurate with the fire, right there onsite. These wildfires are disastrous. They can threaten structures, old-growth trees, and all the vegetation and animal life in the burning area, even down to the microbes. Thousands of people are involved at this level, and the process is even more formal than in a Type 3 fire. When we had one of these fires on the Los Padres, I'd ask the incident commander, "How many of (then governor) Arnold's Schwarzenegger's firefighters did we have to bring in?" We tried to avoid asking these state firefighters for help, because they don't sleep in camp, so we'd have to put them up in motels; they were expensive.

Type 1 and Type 2 fires are true emergency operations, prompting the kind of mobilization that made us a "bureaucratic superstar" in the 1980s.[1] On fires like these, we have timekeepers tracking every single item. Finance people track our contractors and every dollar spent; when you spend five million dollars to put out a fire, you better track every single item! A fire like this requires something like a mini-city to move along with it: we rapidly set up big structures, a massive command fire camp of temporary buildings for each staff unit, such as public affairs, resources, and so on. We have helicopters, twin-engine planes, pilots, and even air traffic controllers. Fighting fire is its own kind of war. No one, except maybe the US military, activates like the Forest Service. That's why our agency was asked to help with cleanup after the space shuttle *Challenger* blew up, and in the aftermath of Hurricane Katrina, and why we have a Homeland Security director; the Forest Service plays an important role in federal emergency response, especially in fire-related organizations and agencies, and that person acts as liaison.

Something is happening all the time on these fires, even at midnight. Any given day, between two hundred and five hundred people are on the fire line during each operational period, with hundreds to thousands more in camp. Not everyone sleeps at the same time on these massive blazes, and personnel don't sleep in motels, including the command staff. Our people doze somewhere in the big field of tents that marks the camp, because anyone and everyone might need to get out on the fire line at any moment. We have commissaries for snacks and provide regular meals and showers onsite. The camp is where firefighters might be able to take a few minutes of down time, a place to relax away from the anxiety of putting your life at risk. Managing forest projects is different than managing fires, where life and death are on the table. This process left me excited and with a heavy sense of responsibility.

Running the Los Padres

I greeted my management team that first day: I told them I looked forward to working with each of them, but I really wanted to meet "the people I will be working for," my employees. They are the most important group on the forest, because if I did my work well for them, they would do the same. I met them and said a few words, and then came the best part, as always—the potluck. That's when I could really connect. I walked around talking with each and every one of the employees. I remember thinking that I needed to remember everyone's name as soon as possible.

The forest mission was to protect watersheds, provide world-class recreation and wilderness opportunities, and provide a living laboratory for ecological diversity and scientific research. The Los Padres had enough space to accomplish these goals and more. People visited for all kinds of reasons, from hiking, biking, and camping to simply communing with nature. The diverse landscape meant five distinct districts to manage with a management team of five staff: Fire Officer Aaron Gelobter and Maeton Freel were in resources; Bruce Emmens ran public uses; Rich Tobin directed international affairs; and Kathy Good guided public affairs. Rangers included Tom Keukes, Mt. Pinos Ranger District; John Bridgewater, Oji RD; Linda Riddle, Santa Barbara RD; Kathleen Phelps, Santa Lucia RD; and John Bradford, Monterey RD.

The best part of working on the Los Padres was that I had a deputy forest supervisor! Gene Blankenship held the job when I arrived, but he had taken his own supervisor's job in Arizona; I had hoped for more of his insight and expertise, but he left just a few weeks after I arrived. Regional foresters hire the forest supervisors and deputies, so a man named Ken Heffner waited in the wings, and I had no say in the decision. As it worked out, I received the best deputy forest supervisor anyone could have. Without Ken my story would end a lot differently. We became partners—he always had my back and he knew I had his. Jane Childers, my incredible assistant, kept all of us in line. Another great thing was that I did not have to start my job by downsizing. I was thrilled! I didn't need to reorganize, and I wouldn't have to go outside the agency seeking money through partnerships. What a stark and pleasant difference from my earlier leadership jobs.

Running the Los Padres meant focusing on more than fire, though. The staff and rangers familiarized me with their district activities, partnerships, and important watershed and wilderness issues like the recovery of the California condor, and provided information on the forest's role as a living laboratory, something that became dear to my heart. This reminded me of Mount St. Helens. It was just the kind of job I loved! They told me I had my work cut out for me: I needed to review projects already in process and make decisions almost immediately. An immediate challenge came from a request to drill oil in the forest. The environmental impact statement for this project had been in process for ten years, and the time came to sign it just as I arrived. I couldn't wait to get home that first night to read the EIS that would inform my decision letter. No rest for the weary! This first California fire day reflected the intensity and pace I faced each and every day, very different from the Siuslaw. I had to hit the ground running hard on the Los Padres, and it was exhilarating. I couldn't wait to get started!

I was pleased to have such a smart and seasoned staff. Some had worked on the forest for years, and Ken and Jane brought insights, education, and experience crucial for the job ahead. After the potluck we went back to my office to decide what came next. We started by filling out my calendar for the entire first month. I had to visit every ranger district to meet employees, and I needed to spend time in the field to see forest-wide issues. We made dates to meet partners and people I should know, like Congresswoman Lois Capps, who was very interested in my oil and gas decision. I went home that first night, exhausted, and read the EIS that had taken ten years to prepare. I was shocked. The forest spent all this time and money for an EIS, just to say the company could drill in the wilderness, for a miniscule amount of oil!

As I reflected on the day, I smiled as I thought about how this first day's experience hadn't been devoted to reading other people's negative body language. All staff and rangers had seemed glad to have me. For once, it really was all about orienting me. I wondered, *Could it have been my own insecurities before, and now it's about my own confidence? Or maybe it's because California forests have experienced more women in leadership positions because of the consent decree?*[2] *Or maybe I feel more comfortable because they have been around people of color before and I'm not so unique.*

Later, I learned about and became part of a cadre of professional women in this part of California, women who shared their knowledge with me. What a relief! Women forest supervisors ran the four Southern California forests. There was Jody Noiron on the Angeles National Forest, near Los Angeles; Tina Terrel at Cleveland, near San Diego; Jeanne Higgins on the San Bernardino; and me. I really liked getting together with these powerful women on a monthly basis to talk. We all dealt with these massive fires, so I didn't feel as alone as I might have, considering fire is traditionally a male domain. We also discussed taking issues before our leadership teams, and addressed local matters that crossed forest boundaries, like the upcoming fire season or budgets. It was really nice, because of the strength in numbers, to get the kind of support we needed. We worked well together, and it didn't take long before we enjoyed a close camaraderie on and off the job. One of our best trips was when Jody took us out on Santa Monica Bay in her motorboat—what a party!

Making Decisions

I soon met with Congresswoman Lois Capps to discuss the oil and gas EIS. She asked whether I'd made a decision. "Not yet," I told her. She felt we should deny the lease, and asked me to tell her the outcome before making it public. I listened, agreed to keep her informed, and returned to the office to meet with the staff. What did they think? How did they conclude that I should sign a decision to allow drilling in the wilderness? They said drilling was already happening in that area, that one more hole wouldn't make a big difference. I didn't think that was good enough. The decision also adhered to our multiple-use mandate, they explained. I shared that, after meeting with Congresswoman Capps, I was between a rock and a hard place. Too often politics played a role in our desire to do a good job and the right thing. My last job had taught me how to finesse around politics and Forest Service. I realized I needed those skills here, too.

I took a few more days and then made a strategic decision. I would permit the lease, but with a restriction. The lessee could not occupy Forest Service land or disturb the wilderness by building roads and setting up camp, because of the environmental impact. I gave a little something to everyone. I told Congresswoman Capps the lease would go through, but the lessee would have to find a way to set up his operation outside of the public lands. He would have to drill diagonally, a very expensive proposition considering the small amount of oil available. The decision satisfied both the congresswoman and my staff, and it pleased me because I knew I'd dodged a bullet. The company decided not to drill. I had also figured out why my staff was so hell-bent on leasing the oil. They had worked on this EIS for a long time, and a lot had happened. It was the early 2000s, the Iraq War still raged, and my staff seemed to feel a patriotic duty to supply oil whenever and wherever they could. I did not. I saw this as a resource grab by the oil industry, not as helping the war effort. It occurred to me that up north I'd had to conserve timber. Here, I would be fighting fire and protecting wilderness. I felt a personal commitment, a duty to defend our environment. I felt very proud.

On my second day, Gene and I went out to see the 10-percent-contained fire, which raged like nothing I'd seen before. I had limited fire knowledge, based on narrow experiences, especially when it came to handling really big fires. I had never had to call for additional help on the Siuslaw. This fire scene burst with activity and people; I had never seen anything like it: tents everywhere, large makeshift dining halls, a Red Cross van, and structures for each resource needed to support the fire. I remember letting Gene take the lead. Everything that day was an intense course on big fire management.

Things had changed by the next big fire. Ken had arrived to show me the guidelines for fire decisions. Everything I knew by the time I left, I learned from him. In the beginning, we visited each fire in the forest together, and he took me step-by-step through my part. He helped me understand and learn fire language and considerations for decision making. I was okay with sharing my lack of knowledge, and he was comfortable telling me whatever I needed to know to make our fire management successful.

California Fires

Not much later, I got a call about a fire on the Santa Lucia Ranger District near Cuyama, then moving toward the San Rafael Wilderness. I called for a Type 1 team, then the Mt. Pinos lightning complex broke out on the Mt. Pinos Ranger District. In a lightning complex, more than one strike occurs, either simultaneously or close together. In this case, the district received more than twenty individual lighting starts in locations close to the Pine Mountain Club community and Frazier Park, both populated areas. With no more Type 1 teams available, and only a Type 2 team up for rotation, we had to figure out what to do. In the field, my fire staff and I discussed rerouting the Type 1 team to the Mt. Pinos District, but the fire staff officer (FSO) on the Santa Lucia dug in his heels. He told people that it was Mt. Pinos' own fault they didn't order a team sooner, and as far as he was concerned, they could rot out there. He wanted the Type 1 team on his district. That's when everyone decided it was time to get me on the phone. I patiently listened to the Santa Lucia FSO, and then

I said, "Let me see if I've got this straight. You're telling me I should not reroute *my* Type 1 team from *your* fire on *my* Santa Lucia District, where no homes are threatened, and that I should continue to send them to the wilderness? You're saying I should not give a damn about *my* Mt. Pinos District that has twenty new fire starts surrounding communities in the middle of the woods? Did I capture that right?"

"Yes ma'am," replied the staff officer.

I said, "I don't have time for this foolishness, and you should know better. Let me tell you what you're going to do."

"Yes ma'am."

"You're going to call dispatch."

"Yes ma'am."

"You are going to make sure they work with South Ops."[3]

"Yes ma'am."

"You're going to let them know we have a higher priority fire on Mt. Pinos, because of the threat to communities."

"Yes ma'am."

"And you're going to get Don Fraiser's team over to the Mt. Pinos District just as soon as you can. Have I made myself clear?"

"Yes ma'am."

I lowered my voice by a few octaves and said, "Thank you, fire staff officer. Is there anything else I can do for you?"

The fire staff officer said, "Uhhh, no ma'am."

"Goodbye," I said. Next, I called dispatch, Don Fraiser, and the ranger, so they heard from me. I realized then that I had developed the confidence to exert real leadership. I knew how to take charge, and I recognized my responsibility to do so. This was a matter of two fires, one affecting wilderness, the other threatening people. I wanted to save wilderness, but I had an even higher duty to protect human communities. It didn't matter if my FSO thought people shouldn't live in these forested areas. They did. We had to shield them, not just from property damage but, potentially, from death. When these California fires burn, they rage. I've seen them jump from one side of a street to another in a matter of moments. They can move tens of miles in an hour. People die. As I write, furious fires are cutting a swath through California communities, killing people and livestock, destroying wild animals and habitat, fires like we've never seen before.

We also tried to deal with fire proactively. Every forest had fuel reduction targets, similar to timber targets, to decrease threats to the urban interface. Every year we exceeded those targets. We set controlled burns that created ground devoid of vegetation to stop fire in its tracks, and it often worked. Prescribed burns helped us reduce our burn unit costs financially, environmentally, and socially. We could burn more acres, reduce fuel buildup, and lower spending, depending on the location. We partnered with Santa Barbara County Fire Department, Bureau of Land Management, and local resident fireshed councils. My decisions about using prescribed burns—from the amount of land, the heat of the burn, and the equipment assigned—ended with good results. But our work did not center only on fire. We had other important programs.

The California Condor and Brazil Ranch

The California Condor Recovery Program also required my attention. By 1967, the federal government knew about the condor's endangerment, and in 1971 the State of California called for protection. Most condors in the wild had been shot, poisoned, or captured, their eggs harvested and their nests disturbed by those resettling the West in mass waves in the nineteenth century. With their food supply severely reduced, these massive vultures moved into the mountains of California, reduced to eating carrion often riddled with toxic lead fragments. Twentieth-century assaults included absorbing DDT, which also made their egg shells so thin they could not reproduce. Their rapidly diminished numbers led scientists to begin a captive breeding program in 1980, capturing all remaining condors and putting them in zoos by mid-decade. When scientists caught the last wild condor in 1987, only twenty-seven of these archaic birds remained in the entire world. At that point, the condor went on the Endangered Species List. It took time, but the captive breeding program worked. The first chick hatched in 1988, and by 1994 the captive condors—birds that live up to forty years—had laid a hundred eggs. In mid-1999, the world held 161 condors, and by 2016, the 446 living condors were hatching twenty babies a year.[4]

My forest aided this process with members of the California recovery plan. We reintroduced the California condor to the wild at our two condor sanctuaries, the 12,000-acre Sisquoc corridor in Santa Barbara

County and our 53,000-acre Sespe corridor in Ventura County. Since birds don't recognize boundaries, we worked with other organizations, like the Fish and Wildlife Service, to save this bird. Maeton Freel took me to meet the birds' caretakers at each of these sanctuaries. Irregular visits allowed us to stay in touch with the program and provided updates on the birds' progress. To me, the condor has to be the ugliest bird in the world—u-g-l-e-e-e-y. It really is a vulture, black, with a bald head sprouting just a few hairlike feathers on top. It has a wingspan of nine and a half feet, with white patches underneath. Yes, it is ugly—until you see it fly. Wow, this bird should qualify for the eighth wonder of the world! When a California condor soars, it becomes awesome, majestic, almost prehistoric. Suddenly the patchy multicolored head doesn't matter; the bird is simply glorious. Every time I saw them, I almost felt for myself the same wonderful mixture of flight and freedom. The bird could slide and glide for hours without flapping its wings. One day, I stood silently, entranced, feeling as if I were witnessing something timeless, beyond special. After what seemed like moments, Maeton told me we had to move on. I was meeting with Rich Tobin, who was responsible for partnerships. We set off for Brazil Ranch.

Brazil Ranch is one of many jewels of the Los Padres, 1,200 acres sitting on a bluff overlooking the Pacific Ocean. After more than a century of ownership, in 1977 the Brazil family sold the ranch to Allen Funt, creator of the television show *Candid Camera*. When Funt died in 1999, developers became interested in the land: they wanted to break it into parcels and build houses, which would have destroyed the character and ambience of this spectacular place. I got to the forest in 2004, in the aftermath of a fight by the community and activists trying to halt the development. With some help from our partnerships department, the Trust for Public Lands purchased Brazil Ranch to preserve it for public use. They donated it to the Forest Service in 2002, and the Los Padres took responsibility for managing this stupendous property, gateway to the Big Sur coast.[5]

The forest put together a board under my supervision, with Rich as my representative, which included Clint Eastwood's wife, Dina Ruiz, a lovely person who treasured the area as much as the locals and who did a lot of volunteer work. She and Clint lived in nearby Carmel on the Monterey Peninsula, where he had saved Carmel's Mission Ranch from development in 1986.[6] A lot of people knew Dina, and her participation raised the board's status, making it easier to recruit others. Eventually the center came to life as a nonprofit, the Big Sur Environmental Institute, with the Los Padres providing educational conservation programs. Since then, the ranch has become a world-class destination meeting place that connects people who come together to discuss environmental issues. Renting the ranch out for these events also brings in revenue for the Forest Service.

I had a chance to meet the caretaker and volunteers who managed this phenomenal place, where restoration has kept the ranch, the barn, and adjacent buildings looking the same as they did a hundred years ago. Couple that with the breathtaking views of the Pacific Ocean and the Big Sur coastline, and it's no wonder that painters, writers, musicians, photographers, and philosophers find it alluring. The media also love it. I loved Brazil Ranch, too, and tried to go there at least once a month. I always left time to visit Monterey, where I loved the shopping almost as much as the scenery! The work on the Los Padres resembled that on the Siuslaw, in that we produced environmental assessments and implemented projects, though I don't remember having timber targets, just burn goals. Everything else centered on wildlife habitat, ecosystem management (e.g., weeds, tree thinning, and so on), wilderness management, and recreation, and we did just about every job alongside partners. Thank goodness I didn't need them to save my budget! As always, we worked with other government agencies, from the US Fish and Wildlife Service to Governor Schwarzenegger's office for fire issues. The Trust for Public Lands played a role here, too, as they did nationally.

Disaster Strikes Again

I loved working with so many people who shared similar ecological values as those we implemented on the forest. The work was fast-paced, with rounds of endless meetings, and I was always on the go. I didn't have time to pay much attention to my own body's messages. One day, seemingly out of the blue, I realized something was wrong. I had been at a fire until around 2:00 a.m. That night, I started to climb the stairs to my second-floor apartment, and then suddenly I couldn't. I was lightheaded, and before fainting I sat down on the bottom step, crying, with no energy to move and wondering what the hell was wrong. I eventually made it up the stairs that night, but the symptoms worsened. I was exhausted, short of breath, and lacked stamina. My job required me to be clearheaded and quick on my feet, but I couldn't concentrate. I felt totally compromised and overloaded.

Finally, my secretary had enough. She made an emergency appointment for me with a local doctor. When the lab sent my results, I learned why everything was so hard. I had chronic lymphoma leukemia. *Cancer? Leukemia? Isn't that the affliction kids get?* The doctor said my white blood cell count was high enough to start therapy. *Start therapy? In California, without Phil? Without my kids?* My world crashed down on me. Before I called my family, I needed more information. "Will this kill me?"

"No."

"What is the therapy?"

"We will start with pills but soon move to chemotherapy."

"What is chemotherapy?" The doctor jargon passed over my head. In my own words, chemotherapy is a liquid poison they pump into a vein to kill off the bad white cells.

Normally, white blood cells are good. They fight off viruses and infection. But with this disease they can exceed the amount needed to protect your body. Then, they become cancerous.

The doctor said, "You could also have side effects."

"Can I work?" He told me that a lot of people do, and it depends.

"I want to be one that works," I said. I went home and called Phil and the kids. The next day, I told my staff, and the day after that I told the RO.

I was determined to keep working, but the therapy made it hard. Phil and Andre came down and insisted that I get a second opinion—in Portland. At the time, the ranger and I were in the middle of seeking an agreement between multiple users for use of the national forest's Santa Barbara Trail—equestrians, bikers, hikers, and, for the winter months, skiers, sledders, and snowmobilers. This agreement was a big deal, and I was critical to the process. I felt a responsibility to deal with it, so I made an appointment with the Oncology Department at Oregon Health and Science University Hospital for two months later. Phil and Andre went back to Portland. I went back to work. But I remained lethargic and depressed, and everything took effort. Exhaustion wrapped over me by the end of each day. After treatment, I would ask the doctor, "When will I get better? When will I be my old self again?" He said we had to keep trying therapies to find one that worked. I still had a meeting every week for a month to complete the trail agreement. *I can only deal with work right now, health be damned*, I thought.

I finally got an arrangement. Each stakeholder had to give up something to use the trail, and no one was completely happy, so I considered it fair. The ranger could work out the remaining details. I still had so much to do! The California off-road vehicle group had problems that we needed to work out forest-wide; the Winchester Canyon Gun Club wanted a permit renewal for their shooting range, and I was getting a lot of complaints from nonmembers that I would have to deal with. First, I had to fly to Portland, meet with my kids and Phil, and get a second opinion from a doctor there. I couldn't believe what I learned—I'd already had leukemia for two years. I was shocked!

When I came to Santa Barbara in 2004, I had found a female internal medicine doctor to be my physician. My Portland consult, Dr. Epps, said that her records showed she had found the leukemia then, in 2004. Now it was November 2006, and she hadn't ever notified me! That was why I had continually felt so sick and sluggish. I'd had leukemia the whole time, and the white cells were multiplying. I was mad. My Portland oncologist at Oregon Health and Science University Hospital suggested a different chemotherapy. I wouldn't die from my disease, he said, but I had a far greater risk for secondary infections than most people. That's what often kills people with leukemia.

An Untimely End

We had some decisions to make. As I moved from one thing to another—work, decisions, doctors, family, Portland, California—I felt I would never catch my breath. I stayed in Portland for two more weeks to try the new chemotherapy. At first, I was sick as hell, but within a few days I felt better than I had for a long time. I sat down with Phil and my kids and we decided that I should transfer back to Portland and receive treatment from Dr. Epps, who clearly knew what he was doing. We agreed that if I could not transfer, I would retire—a painful thought.

When I returned to the Los Padres, Ken and I talked about my plan, and he agreed to do whatever the forest needed. I handed off most of my meetings to him for the rest of the month. Next, I called my boss, the regional forester, Bernie Weingardt. He promised to call Linda Goodman, the regional forester in Portland, to discuss possible work opportunities for me at the Portland RO. Bernie was responsive and supportive, and suggested we request a hardship transfer. I had to write a formal letter to him. He then sent a request to Linda, asking her to find a placement for me. I made a mental note to visit Linda the next time I went to Portland. Then I went about my duties and waited, and waited some more. My next treatment was a month away. If things remained in limbo, I decided I could fly to Portland for my treatment and fly back.

I was so glad to have Dr. Epps! He was great. Cancer patients deal with a lot of needles, and I hate needles, because I have small veins that travel. My doctor understood this. He asked whether I'd like to have something called a PICC[7] inserted into my body, so that I wouldn't have to deal with so many needles. The PICC is a long tube inserted into a large vein that carries blood to the heart. I said, "You want to insert something into my chest? What are you going to do about knocking me out so I don't feel the pain?" The only thing I hated worse than hospitals and needles was pain. But the doctor said he would put me to sleep, so I wouldn't even know, and that's what happened. When I woke up, I had a PICC sticking out from my chest. It was time to return to Santa Barbara. On the plane, I asked myself, *Why I didn't go see Linda like I had planned?* I got that same feeling as when my husband's head hit the steering wheel, a shiver, a chill. *Something is wrong.* The entire trip I tried to figure out why I had avoided going to see Linda, and then it hit me: *If I don't get my transfer, I have to retire. I have to turn in my uniform and my car, and my Forest Service life. I have to pack my house up, hire a delivery company, and move my furniture to Portland. I will have to make all the arrangements and bear all the costs. I will be totally overwhelmed.* As the plane landed, I felt sick, but not because of the cancer.

When I got back to the office, I called Bernie and asked whether he had heard from Linda. Since he hadn't, he suggested that I call her. She had been my regional forester before I went to California, so I had great hope that she would support me. It was time to face the outcome, either way. I was happy and hopeful as could be when she took my call. We said hello, and started a friendly conversation. She asked about Phil, my children, and my work. I told her I loved Santa Barbara and the job. Then I explained that I needed a hardship transfer, so I could take my chemo in Portland. I promised I wouldn't take a lot of time away from the office, that I could work and take treatments. I told her I would take any job, even a "not to exceed" position, which would make it temporary.

Linda sounded very sincere when she said, "I'm sorry, but I just don't have anything for you." She went on to talk about the budget and the difficulty of filling positions. I had stopped listening at "sorry"—I could not believe my ears. How many stories had I heard about the agency facilitating hardship transfers? How many times did we find a job for a guy's wife when he transferred? I was devastated. *I did not want to retire.* I became angry and sad. I could not believe that after thirty-three years of service, I would be forced to retire. I only wanted treatment for my cancer and to be near my family, just like any other hardship case.

Before I left, I had one last job to complete: negotiations with the Winchester Canyon Gun Club, whose permit had expired in 1995. They wanted to legitimize their ongoing use of the property, but the permit had probably been easier to issue twenty years earlier. Now, a lot of activism emerged in opposition to the gun club—complaints about noise, garbage, and lead contamination, the same kind that had affected the condors. I issued a cease-and-desist order to the gun club until we could determine how to address these issues. Why did I think this could happen quickly? We drew up an EA, but community members appealed. We went back to the drawing board. There was significant impact, so we needed an EIS. The process dragged on. Finally, I had to leave this last issue for Ken to resolve.

It was time to return to Portland. My kids came down to help me pack and move my life to a condominium I had purchased two years before, on Corbett Street. I took Andre and his family to see my trail horse, Smokey. The kids wanted more time with Smokey, but we had to leave him for a going-away party held by my staff. It was a sad day: July 4, 2007, my last day of work with the US Forest Service, the agency that had made it possible for me to go from a dictation transcriber to the manager of hundreds of people and more than a million acres. I was grateful for the opportunities I'd had. If I'm honest, I loved the Forest Service. I'd worked hard to get to this place in my life, and had overcome obstacles that most people would never face. I took great pride in knowing I'd made it, and I had done it well. I left my mark on the Forest Service, and it left its mark on me. I mustered up my internal fortitude and headed to the office party, smiling as though retirement had always been my plan.

Community members and many state and local fire people came by to wish me well that day. There were partners and community leaders I had worked with over the previous three years, people I had come to know and like. I was honored that so many came to say goodbye. And then a really funny thing happened. Cell phones started ringing throughout the crowd. One phone and then another, then another. I saw my fire staff officer come toward me and I knew what was happening. There was a fire, and he needed all hands on deck. *How appropriate,* I thought. *When I came to this forest there was a fire, and as I leave there is a fire. Maybe it is time to go home after all.*

Epilogue

THE SONG "TIME OF MY LIFE" sums up my career with the Forest Service. Forest Service took my heart and soul and turned me into someone I could have never imagined. I am grateful for that. Working for the Forest Service was never easy, but it was challenging, rewarding, and, more often than not, a lot of fun! I would say to anyone—woman, person of color, person identifying as LGBTQ, or person with physical challenges— join the Forest Service and splash into a career unlike anything you can imagine. That's what I did.

I showed the Forest Service and western communities that a black woman from Washington, DC, could enter this foreign world and be successful. I believe that my strength did not come from being prideful or powerful, but from a willingness to listen and negotiate when necessary. I came to an agency in transition, in 1974, a new Forest Service that soon incorporated a lot of women and, for the first time, some people of color. The old Forest Service included the white men who joined the agency from the 1940s through the 1970s, those who put timber before all else. These old-time foresters cared for the land through efficient timber harvests and strong relationships with industry and politicians. Their timber programs paid for personnel, vehicles, and everything else, usually to support more timber harvests. But times were changing. My experience in moving through various levels of Forest Service administration taught me that the "serving people" part of our motto was as important as "caring for the land." Serving people meant truly valuing their input and showing it through decision making, while also maintaining the law and reflecting a changing and evolving agency.

The people who live and work in forest communities tend to remain their entire lives. That is why building relationships and transparent communication were the most important parts of my acceptance and success within communities. This was just as true with my coworkers and employees as with environmentalists, industry personnel, ranchers, and politicians. I may not have operated in the same ways as the old-time Forest Service guys, but in the aftermath of the spotted owl controversy, herbicide lawsuits, and diversity efforts, the agency valued communication, relationships, and partnerships like never before. We still required technical expertise and knowledge of lands and ecosystems to make decisions about fish, wildlife, trees, and water. But another important part of the ecosystem had become a priority: people. I may have looked different from old-time foresters, as both a woman and an African American, but I was at the vanguard of this new Forest Service, an organization that needed employees with people skills, not just environmental know-how, one that reflected a broader American population. It turned out that the Forest Service was perfect for me, and I like to think that I was perfect for the Forest Service.

I could have stayed in Washington, DC, and had a decent career, maybe even made GS-11, but I would have never have broken the glass ceiling for African American women if I had stayed. I would have had to raise my children in an urban environment, with fewer possibilities for their futures. The legacies of my career extend beyond my own life, not just through the financial security I provided my children, but also through the opportunities they and their children have had for education, the arts, and exposure to other ways of life. I recognize that my influence also extends beyond the land to the communities I touched and that touched me in turn through interracial friendships and new experiences for us all.

There were times in my career that were less than positive. For example, Montana is where my children learned about racism. When I asked Trina about the details of the fight that resulted in our leaving Missoula, she said, "I don't even want to remember. All of the pre-'nigger' stuff is washed away, because you can't hold on to that kind of hate, and we weren't that kind of family. Better to let it go and move on. It doesn't matter what happened. I lost my sister, my best friend." Our family had never been separated, and we were *very* close. Andre describes our connection through a single moment after Willie James died: I walked into the house with red slippers on and a neck brace, and we all hugged, suddenly fused into "just the four of us."

People in all-white places like Montana knew little to nothing about African American history and had no experience with people of color. They often said things that were embarrassing or insulting. But if you wanted to succeed in a white environment, you had to recognize their responses were based on ignorance, fear, and lack of exposure. Whereas most African Americans had to operate in white environments at least sometimes, many, especially rural, Whites *never* thought about or experienced being the only Caucasian in the room. They didn't know how to act with a few, or even one black person around, much less in communities of color.

Right or wrong, fair or not, black people usually bear the brunt of that lack of familiarity. My philosophy was that if you want to be successful as a black person in a white world, you were the one who had to make it work. That could mean educating white people or simply turning the other cheek. The reality is that many African Americans don't make it past a single summer working for the Forest Service, in part because the onus is always on them. But others do. I'd had to put aside my own feelings and push my way upward. My need to provide a decent life for my children and my own ambition had more power than the words of a few racists.

When I think back, I realize how relieved I felt that the agency helped me deal with my worst-case scenario. I was grateful, but the letter from Dr. Richard Ford, whom I had never met, who did not know me but took the time to reach out personally and share his own feelings about being an outsider in Montana, had comforted me. I later learned that Dr. Ford was an award-winning author and professor at Columbia University. His words helped me to focus on the positive, not the negative, as he wished my family "what's best in the country," rather than exclusion. His empathy provided me with a human connection to someone who recognized my reality, who also felt the insularity of Montana.

As I wrote this memoir, I learned that Professor Ford won a 1996 Pulitzer Prize for his ability to capture both heart-wrenching and beautiful

moments in life,[1] and when I contacted him by email to say how important his letter had been to me, he responded with comforting and honest
words about the current racial environment:

> Being 73 years old, born in Mississippi, being young during the 60s
> civil rights debacles and the putative end of jim crow . . . I always
> say it's just that what was bad before is more visible now. And in a
> way because it's more visible, it's more subject to improvements.
> Obama did a lot, even without fixing all he might've wanted to
> fix. But he brought light to things, which is why we're seeing what
> we're seeing now. *You*, no doubt, always saw it; and I certainly did.
> But many white Americans elected not to. Now racism's in our face
> and harder to deny. Which isn't to say anything's fixed. Perhaps it'll
> never be.[2]

He is right. I had seen it all along. I've also had to rise above it in
order to succeed. Even while writing this book, some of the prejudices
that permeate both the country and the agency continued to affect my
experience, as I received negative feedback for telling my family's truth
about Montana and my own truth about being a black woman in the Forest Service. But my life with the Forest Service and in the West is about far
more than racism or sexism. It is also about overcoming challenges and
coming into my own as a leader and a human being. I loved Montana at
the same time that I hated what it did to my children.

I also loved my Forest Service career. My only regret is that the agency
has not yet achieved the level of diversity that I hoped for as I ended my
career. Fewer people of color work in the Forest Service today than did
in the 1990s, and there have been only two female chiefs, the first for a
single year, the second recently appointed. Increasing and maintaining
diversity in federal agencies takes real commitment by leaders to represent all of American society. Putting a woman or a person of color in
charge does not automatically increase diversity, though it can help. It
takes concerted recruitment and retention efforts and follow-through to
make meaningful change. It takes leaders who understand the need for
agency support systems for those who are different. Creating a diverse
workforce means establishing an environment of acceptance, and it takes

mentors who ensure that employees can obtain the skills they need for success and advancement.

The truth is, the Forest Service made my dreams come true. My goal was to make enough money to support my family, but I received so much more. The Forest Service introduced me to people, places, landscapes, and ideas I could have never imagined. I experienced so many firsts: flying in a plane, riding a horse, peeing in the woods, and making decisions that preserved or altered the natural world, choices made to ensure the health of birds, fauna, flora, fish, wildlife, and the people of our Forest Service districts and communities. My actions and decisions left our public ecosystems in better shape than I found them. This makes me proud. I credit my friends, advisers, and especially my employees for the many opportunities we had to help shape a better world, to make a difference. These people gave me knowledge, advice, friendship, and most importantly, the courage to take risks.

Notes

NOTES TO PREFACE

1   Donna Sinclair, "Caring for the Land, Serving People: The USDA Forest Service in the Civil Rights Era" (unpublished dissertation, Portland State University, 2015).

2   Herbert McLean, "The Regendering of the Forest Service," *Forest World* (Spring 1990): 27.

3   Personal communication, October 2014.

NOTES TO CHAPTER 1

1   The General Schedule (GS) is the pay scale for federal employees, especially those in professional, technical, administrative, or clerical positions. The GS scale ranges from GS-1 to GS-15, with ten steps within each grade; eligibility for GS scale ranges by education and experience. Comparing GS levels to military rank, GS-9 is similar to a low-level officer, while GS-15 compares with a colonel or a captain. Individuals at the executive level, like the Forest Service chief or associate chiefs, must qualify for the senior executive service, which used to be identified as levels GS-16, 17, and 18. For information about series and grades in the US government, see USA Jobs at https://www.usajobs.gov/Help/faq/pay/series-and-grade/.

2   Men averaged a 9.88 GS level service-wide in 1978, and women averaged 5.91. As late as 1989, most women in the agency averaged GS-6.6, with men still nearly three points higher. USDA Forest Service, Human Resources and Personnel Management, 1980 Workforce Planning Data Book, in Donna Sinclair, "Caring for the Land, Serving People: The USDA Forest Service in the Civil Rights Era" (unpublished dissertation, Portland State University, 2015), p. 19.

3   "Come and Get These Memories," Metrolyrics website, http://www.metrolyrics.com/come-and-get-these-memories-lyrics-the-supremes.html, accessed October 3, 2015.

4   "District of Columbia Crime Index Rates per One Hundred Thousand Inhabitants," prepared by the Disaster Center, http://www.disastercenter. com/crime/dccrime.htm, accessed April 28, 2016.

5   Campbell Gibson and Kay Jung, "Historical Census Statistics on Population Totals by Race, 1970 to 1990, and by Hispanic Origin, 1970 to 1990, for the United States, Regions, Divisions, and States," Working Paper Series No. 56, September 2002. Detailed tables, by state, available at http:// www.census.gov/population/www/documentation/twps0056/twps0056. html.

NOTES TO CHAPTER 2

1   Norman Maclean, *A River Runs Through It and Other Stories* (University of Chicago Press, 1976), p. 215.

2   Gerald Williams, "Women in the Forest Service," USDA Forest Service, Rocky Mountain Region website, https://www.fs.usda.gov/detail/r2/ learning/history-culture/?cid=stelprdb5360500, accessed May 21, 2019.

3   Agency employment remained stable at around twenty thousand full-time employees from 1958 to 1980, rising to thirty-two thousand by 1992. Donna Sinclair, "Caring for the Land, Serving People: The USDA Forest Service in the Civil Rights Era" (unpublished dissertation, Portland State University, 2015), pp. 226, 351.

4   "Shades of Racism: A Black Family Reflects on a Year in Missoula," *Missoulian*, July 21, 1987.

5   "The Bob Marshall Wilderness," Wilderness Connect website, http:// www.wilderness.net/NWPS/wildView?WID=64, accessed November 23, 2017.

6   Timothy Egan, *The Big Burn: Teddy Roosevelt and the Fire That Saved America* (New York: Mariner Books, 2010), p. 166.

7   See Egan, *Big Burn*, pp. 158–171.

8   The Wilderness Act, Public Law 88-577 (16 USC 1131-1136), 88th Congress, 2nd Session, September 3, 1964.

9   "Shades of Racism," p. 1.

10   Sinclair, "Caring for the Land, Serving People," p. 367.

11   Sinclair, "Caring for the Land, Serving People," p. 403.

12   Personal communication, 2018.

NOTES TO CHAPTER 3

1   "Biography," Margaret Carter Oral History Interview by Janice Dilg, April 18, 2016. Oregon State University Sesquicentennial Oral History

Project, http://scarc.library.oregonstate.edu/oh150/carter/biography.html.

2 See Gregory Nokes, *Breaking Chains: Slavery on Trial in the Oregon Territory* (Corvallis: Oregon State University Press, 2013).

3 Donna Sinclair, "Caring for the Land, Serving People: The USDA Forest Service in the Civil Rights Era" (unpublished dissertation, Portland State University, 2015), p. 417.

4 Sinclair, "Caring for the Land, Serving People," Table 5: Number of Employees, 1984–2011, p. 33.

5 Sinclair, "Caring for the Land, Serving People," p. 389.

6 According to Michael Milstein and Phil Roni, scientists from the Northwest Fisheries Science Center have shown that large logs and rootwads play a natural role in most river systems, and wood placed in rivers can improve habitat conditions "by creating pools and providing cover. Wood also increases the retention of organic matter and nutrients and helps create islands and new channels that provide additional refuge and habitat, especially for rearing juvenile fish." Milstein and Roni, "Findings Offer New Guidance for Effective Restoration Projects," Northwest Fisheries Science Center, January 2015, https://www.nwfsc.noaa.gov/news/features/woody_debris/index.cfm.

7 Mike Kerrick, interview by Gloria Brown and Donna Sinclair, October 28, 2014, Springfield, Oregon. In authors' possession.

8 See https://www.fs.usda.gov/main/planningrule/history for the history of the planning rule.

9 *Citizens Against Toxic Sprays, Inc. v. Bergland*, 428 F. Supp. 908 (D. Or. 1977), US District Court for the District of Oregon - 428 F. Supp. 908 (D. Or. 1977), March 7, 1977, https://law.justia.com/cases/federal/district-courts/FSupp/428/908/1792293/; Lawrence and Mary Rakestraw, *History of the Willamette National Forest* (USDA Forest Service, Pacific Northwest Region, 1991), https://foresthistory.org/wp-content/uploads/2017/01/HISTORY-OF-THE-WILLAMETTE-NATIONAL-FOREST.pdf.

NOTES TO CHAPTER 4

1 "Willamette National Forest," USDA Forest Service website, https://www.fs.usda.gov/main/willamette/about-forest, accessed December 28, 2017.

2 The Forest Service Union is the National Federation of Federal Employees, Affiliated with the International Association of Machinists and Aerospace Workers, AFL-CIO. For more information, see http://www.nffe-fsc.org/.

3   "The Forest Service is required by statute to have a national planning
    rule: the Forest and Rangeland Renewable Resources Planning act of
    1974, as amended by the National Forest Management Act of 1976, re-
    quires the Secretary of Agriculture to issue regulations under the prin-
    ciples of the Multiple-Use Sustained-Yield Act of 1960 for the develop-
    ment and revision of land management plans," USDA Forest Service
    website, "The Forest Planning Rule," https://www.fs.usda.gov/detail/
    planningrule/faqs/?cid=stelprdb5270279, accessed March 23, 2018.

4   USDA Forest Service, *Federal Advisory Committee on the Implementa-
    tion of the 2012 Land Management Planning Rule, A Citizens' Guide to
    National Forest Planning* (June 2016), p. 9, https://www.fs.usda.gov/In-
    ternet/FSE_DOCUMENTS/fseprd509144.pdf.

5   USDA Forest Service, *Citizens' Guide*, p. 11.

6   1982 Rule, National Forest System Land and Resource Management
    Planning, September 30, https://www.fs.fed.us/emc/nfma/includes/
    nfmareg.html#Public%20participation.

7   Gerald W. Williams, *The US Forest Service in the Pacific Northwest: A
    History* (Corvallis: Oregon State University Press, 2009), p. 273. FOR-
    PLAN had served as the primary analysis tool for Forest Service land
    management planning since 1980, and its capabilities and limitations are
    well documented. Problems after a critique of FORPLAN led Forest Ser-
    vice to develop a different tool called Spectrum; Kendrick Greer and
    Bruce Meneghin, "Spectrum: An Analytical Tool for Building Natural
    Resource Management Models," https://www.ncrs.fs.fed.us/pubs/gtr/
    other/gtr-nc205/pdffiles/p53.pdf.

8   "Jeff DeBonis," LinkedIn, https://www.linkedin.com/in/jeff-debonis-
    b4975635/, accessed January 5, 2018.

9   "Whistleblower Protection Act: An Overview," FindLaw, http://employ-
    ment.findlaw.com/whistleblowers/whistleblower-protection-act-an-
    overview.html, accessed March 5, 2018.

10 The Forest Service Employees for Environmental Ethics website, https://
    www.fseee.org/, accessed January 8, 2018.

11 Gerald W. Williams, *The U.S. Forest Service in the Pacific Northwest: A
    History* (Corvallis: Oregon State University Press, 2009), p. 371.

12 Sinclair, "Caring for the Land, Serving People," p. 21.

13 John C. Hendee, George H. Stankey, and Robert C. Lucas, *Wilderness
    Management*, Miscellaneous Publication No. 1365, October 1978 (US
    Department of Agriculture Forest Service), https://www.fs.fed.us/cdt/
    carrying_capacity/wilderness_management_misc_pub_1365.pdf.

14 The Wilderness Act of 1964, Public Law 88-577 (16 USC 1131-1136),
    88th Congress, 2nd Session (September 3, 1964), as amended, https://
    www.wilderness.net/nwps/legisact.

15 Hendee et al., *Wilderness Management*, p. 4.

16 The population in 2010 was 3,205. "Oakridge, Oregon Population: Census 2010 and 2000 Interactive Map, Demographics, Statistics, Quick Facts," Census Viewer, http://censusviewer.com/city/OR/Oakridge, accessed September 7, 2018.

NOTES TO CHAPTER 5

1 Donna Sinclair, "Caring for the Land, Serving People: The USDA Forest Service in the Civil Rights Era" (unpublished dissertation, Portland State University, 2015), p. 369.

2 Bureau of Land Management Facts, https://www.blm.gov/nhp/facts/, accessed May 2, 2018.

3 As of 2013, federal lands constituted nearly 53 percent of Oregon's lands (ca. 33 million acres) and 28.5 percent of Washington's (ca. 12 million acres); "Federal Land Ownership by State," *Ballotpedia*, https://ballotpedia.org/Federal_land_ownership_by_state, accessed May 7, 2018.

4 These lands had been formerly owned by railroads but were returned to the government after major land fraud prosecutions in the early twentieth century, leaving the General Land Office and then the BLM with significant timber management responsibilities. "Jeff LaLande, US Bureau of Land Management," Oregon Encyclopedia, https://oregonencyclopedia.org/articles/u_s_bureau_of_land_management/#.WvCKR4gvy00, accessed May 4, 2018.

5 William Ashworth, "Hells Canyon: Man, Land, and History in the Deepest Gorge on Earth," American Heritage 28, no. 3 (April 1977), https://www.americanheritage.com/content/hells-canyon.

6 Bureau of Land Management, Public Lands Foundation for America's Heritage, "America's Public Lands: Origins, History, Future," December 2014 (Arlington, VA: Public Lands Foundation), p. 5, https://publicland.org/wp-content/uploads/2016/08/150359_Public_Lands_Document_web.pdf.

7 Email correspondence, Dave Hunsaker to Gloria Brown, May 2018.

8 See Elliott West, *The Last Indian War: The Nez Perce Story* (Oxford: Oxford University Press, 2011).

9 West, *Last Indian War*, pp. 296, 301–330.

10 US Department of Interior, Bureau of Land Management, Baker Field Office, Draft Resource Management Plan and Environmental Impact Statement, volume 3, prepared by Baker Resource Area, Vale District, October 2011, https://www.blm.gov/or/districts/vale/plans/bakerrmp/files/Vol3_Baker_DEIS-RMP.pdf.

NOTES TO CHAPTER 6

1   "Mount St. Helens," USDA Gifford Pinchot National Forest website, https://www.fs.usda.gov/main/giffordpinchot/learning, accessed June 5, 2018.

2   US Geological Survey, "Cataclysmic 1980 Eruption," https://volcanoes. usgs.gov/volcanoes/st_helens/st_helens_geo_hist_99.html, accessed July 13, 2018.

3   *Columbian*, October 23, 1997, p. E1.

4   "Mount St. Helens Visitor Center," Washington State Parks website, https://parks.state.wa.us/245/Mount-St-Helens, accessed July 9, 2018.

5   "State to Take Over Mount St. Helens Visitor Center," *Daily Chronicle*, June 21, 2007, http://www.chronline.com/news/state-to-take-over-mount-st-helens-visitor-center/article_00281601-31d7-5659-9209-a97d-2b01939a.html.

6   Gerald W. Williams, "National Monuments and the Forest Service," USDA Forest Service, November 18, 2003, https://www.nps.gov/parkhistory/online_books/fs/monuments.htm.

7   The Cooperative Education Program provides job experiences during summers while students work for the Forest Service during the academic year.

8   "Mission and History," Mount St. Helens Institute website, http://mshinstituteold.presencehost.net/about_us/, accessed August 9, 2018. The "History" section of this website notes that the institute began in 1996, but it did not obtain funding and 501(c)(3) status until after the taskforce determined how to move forward.

NOTES TO CHAPTER 7

1   Leslie Weldon interview by Tania McDonnell, May 11, 2005, Bend, Oregon. Forest Service Civil Rights Collection.

2   Siuslaw National Forest website, https://www.fs.usda.gov/main/siuslaw/home, accessed August 27, 2018.

3   Save the Oregon Dunes website, https://www.saveoregondunes.org/, accessed August 27, 2018.

4   Jim Furnish, *Toward a Natural Forest: The Forest Service in Transition, A Memoir* (Corvallis: Oregon State University Press, 2015), pp. 115, 117.

5   Catrina almost died from heart failure again in the fall of 2015. Her first donated heart was shutting down, and Oregon Health and Science University did not think they could find another heart in time. She also needed a special proprietary treatment to clear away antibodies that could harm the new heart, and the treatment was available only at Ce-

dars-Sinai Hospital in Los Angeles. We put Catrina on a plane with a nurse and I drove down. The treatment over the next nine months damaged her kidneys, and she had to go on dialysis. The weaker she got, the more afraid I got. I was going back and forth to the hospital until she became deathly ill. Then I got a bed in her room. When I was sure she was asleep, I cried in my pillow. I could see her getting weaker and weaker.

In March 2016 her new heart and kidney arrived, both from the same donor. She was in the hospital two more months before being released to go home to Portland. My daughter is the bravest spiritual person I know. Every day she gives more than she receives.

6 Michael Milstein, "Cutting the Controversy," *Oregonian*, March 14, 2004, p. A15.

7 For more on the Siuslaw during the 1990s, see Furnish, *Toward a Natural Forest.*

8 Michael Milstein, "Order Bars 170 Sales of Timber in Region," *Oregonian*, December 9, 2000, p. E01.

9 Groups I dealt with included Earthjustice, the Sierra Club, the Trust for Public Lands, and the Audubon Society.

10 Gloria Brown, "Decades of Change ... A Challenge for the Future," Siuslaw National Forest website, https://www.fs.usda.gov/detail/siuslaw/landmanagement/planning/?cid=fsbdev7_007192, accessed November 3, 2018.

11 National Forest Foundation website, https://www.nationalforests.org/who-we-are, accessed October 5, 2018.

NOTES TO CHAPTER 8

1 Jeannie Nienaber and Daniel C. McCool, *Staking Out the Terrain: Power and Performance among Natural Resource Agencies* (Albany: State University of New York, 1995).

2 In 1972, Gene Bernardi, a GS-11 female sociologist at the Pacific Southwest Station in Region 5, filed an EEO claim based on sexual discrimination regarding her position description. Following her challenge, by 1977, a class-action lawsuit resulted in two consent decrees in California and forced the entire agency to rethink its hiring and promotion practices. Carla Fisher, "You're Not Getting Rid of Me: Cultivating Space for Women in the U.S. Forest Service, 1950–1990" (unpublished dissertation, Purdue University, 2010), p. 64.

3 This refers to fire operations in southern California.

4 "California Condor," California Department of Fish and Wildlife, https://www.wildlife.ca.gov/Conservation/Birds/California-Condor, accessed November 14, 2018.

5   "Brazil Ranch, Guided Hikes," Los Padres National Forest website, April 13, 2006, http://bigsurcalifornia.org/images2/06images/06-04-12Brazil-RanchROG.pdf.
6   Jake Rossen, "30 Years Ago Clint Eastwood Was Elected Mayor of Carmel, California," April 7, 2016, http://mentalfloss.com/article/78257/30-years-ago-clint-eastwood-was-elected-mayor-carmel-california.
7   Peripherally inserted central catheter.

NOTES TO EPILOGUE

1   Dr. Richard Ford won the Pulitzer Prize in 1996 for his book, *Independence Day*, http://www.pulitzer.org/winners/richard-ford, accessed October 17, 2017.
2   Email from Dr. Richard Ford to Gloria Brown, 2017.

Index